GRAND SLAM

AN INSIDE LOOK AT MAJOR LEAGUE BASEBALL

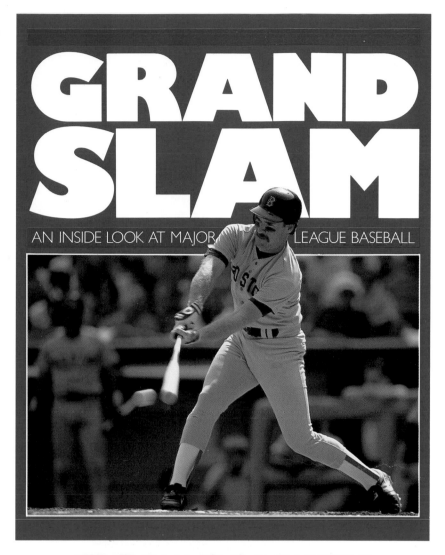

TEXT BY ANGUS G. GARBER III
PHOTOGRAPHS BY JOHN McDONOUGH

Friedman Group

ISBN 0-8317-3958-4

GRAND SLAM: An Inside Look at Major League Baseball
was prepared and produced by
Michael Friedman Publishing Group, Inc.
15 West 26th Street
New York, NY 10010

Editor: Bruce Lubin
Designer: Robert W. Kosturko
Photo Editor: Christopher Bain
Production Manager: Karen Greenberg

Typeset by BPE Graphics, Inc.
Color separations by South Sea International Press Ltd.
Printed and bound in Hong Kong by Leefung-Asco Printers Ltd.

Author's Dedication

For the Eliots, Kate and John

Photographer's Dedication

For my family

Acknowledgments

Deep appreciation to those who gave their time to this effort, especially Claire Smith of the *Hartford Courant*, who understands baseball as keenly as the people who play it; the ballplayers who endured hours of tedious questions and produced some memorable answers; *Courant* colleague Steve Fainaru, for his delicious anecdotes; the *Newark Star-Ledger*'s Moss Klein and Dan Castellano; the public relations men of the major leagues, particularly the Yankees' Harvey Greene; umpire Steve Palermo; Ted Giannoulas, a.k.a. "The Famous Chicken;" Joseph Reichler, for his amazing *Baseball Encyclopedia;* those purveyors of numbers at the Elias Sports Bureau; Bruce Lubin of the Michael Friedman Publishing Group; and my wife, Gerry, for her patience.

Introduction · 6

CONT

E N T S

Introduction

More than any other sport, baseball is simply a game: The players wear caps and stockings and chase a ball in lush, green pastures. It is the only major sport where you won't find a clock; if the game is tied after nine innings, a result is determined in extra innings. Ominous terms like *sudden death* and *overtime* need not apply.

In football, hockey, and basketball, the age of thirty generally represents the line of demarcation. But because there are no mind numbing tackles (with the rare exception of a batter who has been wronged by an inside fastball and chooses to deliver his personal message to the man who threw it), no vicious slashes or cross-checks from a wickedly dangerous

stick, no endless runs up and down a hardwood court that reduce knees and ankles to mush, some of baseball's heroes enjoy productive seasons into their late thirties and beyond. As the Mets' Lee Mazzilli said when he turned thirty-two, "Girls used to come up to me and tell me, 'My sister loves you.' Now they say, 'My mother loves you.' "

For instance: How long would Joe Namath or Wilt Chamberlain have lasted if they had played 162 games a year? Baseball schedules nearly *twice* as many games as any other sport each season. It also places greater emphasis on the thought process. The well-traveled Mike Easler taps his head and says, "It's all where your cabeza is." Notes Ken Griffey, a career .300 hitter, "Baseball is 98 percent mental. It comes down to that moment when the ball comes in. You say either, 'I can hit it,' or 'I'm not going to hit it.' You decide."

Is it a coincidence that laid back California traditionally produces more professional baseball players than any other state? It is an offbeat game that embraces some strange customers. Lawrence Peter Berra is the touchstone there. This five-foot-seven, 185-pound catcher wreaked more havoc with the English language than with his American League opponents. Yogi played on ten (count them, ten)

New York Yankees championship teams, yet he is best known for his pithy philosophy of "It ain't over till it's over." Though Yogi grew up with fellow catcher and announcer-to-be Joe Garagiola in St. Louis, he exuded baseball's inherent *laissez-faire* mindset. This, after all, is the sport that gave us Bill Lee. He was a left-handed pitcher—that was his political leaning, too—from Burbank, California, called "Spaceman" by his teammates. And, with good reason. Lee won 119 major league games before retiring in 1982, but he ran for President in 1988 on the little known Rhinoceros Party ticket. His platform: "I'll live in Washington and I'll be President and pitch for the [defunct] Washington Senators. I'll bring baseball back to the city. It'll be a law." And: "We have lots of ideas. One is that you'll stay in shape. If you're walking down the street and you're out of shape, a van pulls up and three burly guys grab you. You're shipped to basic training for eight weeks. Where's Dad? He's out of shape and away for eight weeks. It's all right. He'll be back a new person."

Remember Pascual Perez, the Atlanta pitcher who broke the tension of a 1982 losing streak that mushroomed to 19 defeats in 21 games? Perez had just been traded by the Pittsburgh Pirates and was scheduled to pitch when he got lost on the way to Atlanta Fulton County Stadium. He spent most of the night circling the city on Route 285, missing his start and running out of gas. When the Braves eventually won the National League West title, they pointed to Perez's dubious navigational skills as the key to the season; he unwittingly changed the course of a potentially disastrous slide.

Former pitcher Jim Bouton opened the private world of the clubhouse forever in 1970 with his book *Ball Four.* In it, we discovered that baseball players were people, too. We learned that the Yankee's Joe Pepitone was the first man to bring a hair dryer into the locker room, Mickey Mantle occasionally liked to sample the nectar of the gods, and George Brunet, who pitched for ten different teams in a fifteen-year career, declined to wear underwear for any of them.

Baseball, as Garagiola himself has written, is a funny game. How to explain one George Steinbrenner? The Yankees' owner has an ego larger than all of New York; in 1981 he ordered 50,000 copies of the Yankees yearbook removed from the concession stands because he didn't like his photograph. This is the man who hired Billy Martin *five*

7

different times to manage his ball club. Yet it is men like Steinbrenner who allow baseball to exist in this purest of forms. Beer baron August Busch, owner of the St. Louis Budweisers, uh, Cardinals, is said to be worth $1.3 billion. San Diego Padres owner Joan Kroc, whose late husband Ray founded McDonald's, is another billionaire. Ted Turner, the television mogul, owns the Atlanta Braves, and Tom Monaghan, the brains behind Domino's Pizza, calls Detroit's Tigers his own. Sure, baseball is a wise investment and a terrific tax write-off, but sometimes a guy just likes to hang around the batting cage.

Where else can you see guys who make as much as $2 million a year scramble for cold cuts, potato salad, and fried chicken—on paper plates—after they get off work? Or players refuse to wash their uniforms when the team is on a hot streak? During the summer of 1987, the Salt Lake

Trappers of the Class A Pioneer League won 29 straight games, a professional baseball record. Their secret? No player washed his socks, and some washed nothing at all, during the winning streak. Although not one opponent accused them of playing dirty, for the sake of public comfort someone probably should have.

Baseball is where men hide while the world grows up around them. Listen to Kansas City outfielder Willie Wilson, who weathered a messy divorce in 1986 and saw his batting average dip to .269: "It's easy to play when you're happy. It's a different story when you have a lot of distractions. Every day I came into the clubhouse there were messages on my chair. Call this lawyer, call that lawyer. You never knew what awaited you. This spring, I just come into the clubhouse and start messing around with the fellows. The only thing I worry about now is getting my furniture back."

The Baseball Experience

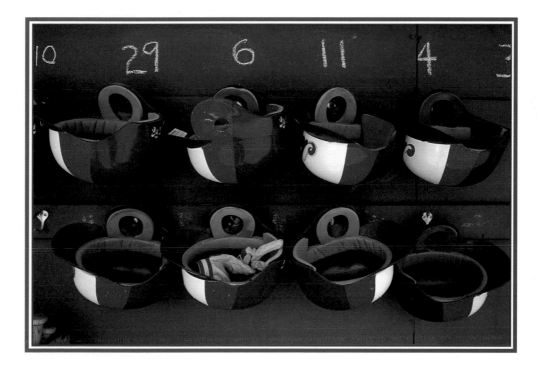

Spring Training

Spring is, for the game of baseball, a hopeful time. Every February, baseball's 26 teams head for Florida and Arizona, where optimism just ricochets around those diamonds with the velocity of a Nolan Ryan fastball. It can leave you giddy. Really. There are no ugly losses yet, no debilitating injuries, so every team looks good. Why, players are even happy to see baseball writers. There is a nice blend of veterans and promising rookies here, the manager notes as he leans on the back of the batting cage, checking out the rays. Hitting, a problem last season, is sure to be better this year. And the pitching, he says, should be improved with the acquisition of so-and-so. I mean, is it possible to have too much pitching? Only in spring training.

In 1888 the Washington Statesmen, who had a catcher named Connie Mack, became the first team to train in the Sunshine State. That's a hundred years of tradition. Maybe it's the warm weather in the Grapefruit and Cactus Leagues—it has a gentle effect on aging hamstrings and young psyches—or perhaps the idea of starting over. Everything happens s-l-o-w-l-y. With any luck at all the season won't end until October, some eight months hence, so there is no reason to rush around. Instead, hone that new off-speed pitch, work on that suntan. Veterans, who like to walk around with their caps off, will tell you that a good tan can make you look ten pounds lighter, an important consideration for those in danger of deportation to the minor leagues. Rookies don't yet understand this. They take it all far too seriously. "It's not the way it was when I first came up," says pitcher John Candelaria, whose rapidly graying hair is the result of his doing this for sixteen seasons. "I was trying to throw it by the starters, trying to prove to the manager that I belonged here. You've got to pace yourself. Now I see the situation reversed. I'm just trying to get my arm going, and these kids come in here and

SPRING TRAINING, FOR ALL
*its lyrical grace, is a struggle at
times. For some reason, managers
insist on annual proof that the old
guys can still do it. Cincinnati's
Pete Rose (below) was always in
midseason form—even in March.*

try to blow everybody away."

Spring training is about relearning, which explains some of the drudgery. See the pitching staff lined up on the mound as the coach rolls a baseball down the third-base line. Just as the pitcher deftly scoops it up, the coach shouts "second base," and the athlete wheels and delivers the ball . . . into center field. He will do it again and again (and again) until he gets it right, so some announcer in late summer can say after a particularly well-executed play off the mound, "Well, Vern, that's why they work on that play in spring training." Through repetition, the theory goes, the correct reflexes will become automatic. Meanwhile, batters toughen up the calluses on their hands. There is also running, lots of running in the outfield. Baseball players are not the world's most finely conditioned athletes, and a little enforced hard labor is usually necessary if those alarming numbers on the scale in the trainer's room are to be dealt with. Some players even lift weights.

Do not get the impression, however, that spring training is an entirely grim enterprise. Far from it. The players arrive at the clubhouse around nine in the morning, grab a cup of coffee, and shoot the breeze for an hour while they get dressed. Anyone with a chance to make the big club is invited to spring training, and that makes for a lot more conversational victims than the team will take north. There are a lot of extra instructors, too. Some former stars like to stretch the old uniform over their thickening bodies and play ball again. They're the ones with the set of golf clubs in their lockers. Workouts usually last two or three hours, and sometime after noon, the players are on their own. Most of them live in apartments near the training facility and spend the afternoon with the family at the beach, or playing golf with teammates. It's almost a vacation.

PLAYERS PONDER THE future during spring training: Can I still hit the slider on the outside corner, or get to the ball in the gap? It's also a time for them to appreciate the physical beauty of Arizona or Florida. Not until August, in the heat of a pennant race, does tunnel vision set in.

The games begin in early March and no one much cares who wins. They are played in minor-league parks in places like Chain O'Lakes Park in Winter Haven, Florida, Ho Ho Kam Park in Mesa, Arizona, and Osceola Stadium in Kissimmee, Florida. The ticket prices at some parks, like Fort Lauderdale Stadium, home of the New York Yankees—$9 for a box seat, $7.50 for reserved, and $4 for admission to the bleachers—approach the regular-season tariff. But then again, the view in these intimate parks is priceless:

Underneath the stands in Fort Lauderdale, Yankees coach Jeff Torborg is in a familiar position. He's squatting in the dust behind a plate, sizing up a prospect. Torborg played catcher for the Los Angeles Dodgers and California Angels for ten seasons and, along the way, caught no-hitters thrown by Sandy Koufax, Bill Singer, and Nolan Ryan. So he knows a little bit about pitching. Anyway, the prospect is just burning them in there. He's been in the game one year and he already has a shot at Double-A ball if things go well down here.

The ball arrives precisely where Torborg's glove is set up and he says, "Great pitch. Now it's one-and-two. What are you going to follow that fastball with?"

The prospect squirms and says, "A changeup, I think."

The motion says fastball, but the pitch comes in like a medicine ball. The imaginary hitter, way ahead, swings early and misses. "Perfect!" Torborg exalts. "Struck him out." Torborg is supposed to be unbiased, but this left-hander from the Pittsburgh organization is his all-time favorite. It is his son, Doug. How good will he be?

"Great," Torborg proudly whispers, so his son won't hear. "I could take him into a major league game right now. And I'm not saying it because he's my boy. He's got great stuff."

Out on the field, New York Yankee pitchers Ron Guidry and Dave Righetti

and slugger Mike Pagliarulo are cavorting with blue and white Yankees umbrellas for a television producer. "Just singing in the rain," they croon, deftly twirling the umbrellas. "What a glorious feeling . . ." Later in the season, this off-key piece of work will help promote Umbrella Day. In a few hours, Guidry will offer a solo for his teammates in the clubhouse. Since no eggs or tomatoes are handy, Guidry is bombarded with a shower of dirty socks and jocks.

Under owner George Steinbrenner's reign of terror, the players are kept very much in line. The sign on the clubhouse bulletin board explains the boundaries. For instance: "1. Personal Grooming—Hair neat, well-groomed. No long hair. No mutton chops or long

sideburns. Moustaches must be trimmed—no moustache below lower lip. No beards." There are dire warnings about bringing salesmen or children into the clubhouse, wearing T-shirts while traveling, and so on. *Glasnost* has not yet arrived in Steinbrenner's narrow world view.

Up the road a bit, in West Palm Beach, it is still baseball as usual. The fans are a tad excited here this season, where some of the Montreal Expos' pitchers are working on their first-base coverage. The folks actually applaud when Randy St. Claire successfully beats a runner to the bag. On another field, the players are running through a drill that looks curiously like football. The quarterback takes the snap from center and lofts a base-

ball to the streaking wide receiver, who catches the ball bare-handed. Naturally, this is the players' favorite drill. The Expos share the complex with the Atlanta Braves, who dress under the stands behind first base. The sign on the wall authored by a Braves clubhouse man sums up the attitude of those who work with the teams: "Put your wet stuff in the hampers every day, or you will be shot!"

Up the east coast is Port St. Lucie, a town that spent more than $11 million on a new complex and wooed the 1986 world champion New York Mets from St. Petersburg.

Here are the Mets, up close and personal. The fans buzz around with cameras. Click, click. It's an exclusive photo of Ken Dowell, who may or may

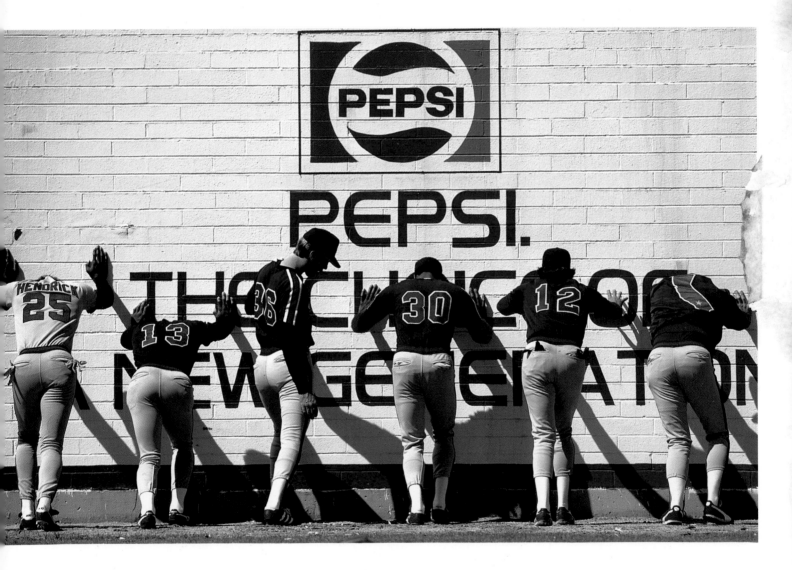

SEE THE CALIFORNIA AN-gels yawn. See them stretch their $500,000 hamstrings against the wall. There is time for everything now, a chat in the dugout or an autograph for a fan. Sometimes, even hitting takes a back seat to baseball talk.

not play in Triple-A ball this year. Suitable, of course, for framing.

The Kansas City Royals have just pulled up stakes themselves. After nineteen years in Fort Myers, the Royals moved into a $13 million facility twenty-five miles from Orlando that is modestly called Baseball City. In truth, it is a huge amusement park. The town fathers are aware that the eighteen baseball teams in Florida and their fans spend nearly $300 million each brief spring season.

The Dodgers work in Vero Beach, where today a group of Russian coaches is observing their training methods. "We want to learn everything," says Guela Chikhradze, assistant coach of the U.S.S.R. national team. "In America, baseball is number one sport. The Dodgers are an old and famous club. This will help us." Some of the Dodgers giggle as the Soviets go through awkward contortions. They are a little rough around the edges right now, but wait until 1992, when baseball becomes a medal sport in the Olympics.

The Dodgers are very good at foreign relations; a few days earlier the Chunichi Dragons of Japan came to visit. Their accommodations were marvelous because Dodgertown is a self-contained entity. Back in the late 1940s, after he made Jackie Robinson major-league baseball's first black player, Branch Rickey was unhappy with the reception Vero Beach gave Robinson and his teammate, Roy Campanella. They weren't welcome in movie theaters or laundromats, so Rickey built his own facility: Dodgertown. There are barracks for the young players, bungalows for the married men, tennis courts, two golf courses, and a movie house. The entire organization works here during the spring, and it truly is a sight to see. Hope springs eternal in each breast wrapped in Dodger Blue.

Is it possible to have too much pitching? Only in spring training.

The Ballpark

Part of baseball's timeless nature, the thing that makes it so completely different from other sports, derives from the fields it is played upon: The game literally knows no consistent boundaries. This is important.

Instead of the cold, prescribed dimensions of rectangular football fields, basketball courts, or hockey rinks, the baseball field is the park it's played in. Yankee Stadium, an elegant monument to the glory days of Ruth and Gehrig, would be impossible to reconstruct in this era of horribly homogeneous multipurpose stadiums. If a right-handed batter jumps on the fastball and pulls it directly down the left-field line, he can park one in the seats only 318 feet away. If he's a little

late, he pays the price: it's 379 to left field, 399 to left-center, and 408 to dead-center field. It could be worse. Prior to 1976, the distance was 461 feet to center and 457 to left-center. Consider the odd measure of Boston's Fenway Park. It's a reasonable 315 feet down the left-field line, but you have to scale the fourteen-foot "Green Monster" and the twenty-three-foot screen to knock one out. Though the center-field corner is a distant 420 feet away from home plate, a hitter can curl a modest 302-foot hit around the foul pole in right field and collect all four bases. Some players who have paced it off themselves claim the actual distance is more like 295 feet. The average dimensions of a big-league

park, however, are 330 feet to left and right and 405 feet to center.

The majors' twenty-six parks are divided into three basic categories: 1) lovable, eccentric relics, 2) the sanitized, symmetrical venues of the 1970s, 3) modern domed stadiums where baseball is criminally played indoors with all the charm of outdoor plumbing. If Abner Doubleday, the nineteenth-century U.S. Army officer who is generally credited with inventing the game, were permitted to see his creation played in any of the so-called parks that fall into these latter two groups, he'd probably sue for fraud. The common denominator of the first group is, simply, grass. As slugger Richie Allen once said of arti-

WHETHER IT'S A BREWERS-Twins game at Milwaukee Stadium (left) or batting practice at Candlestick Park, baseball is just another day at the office. But this office is outside—and that's where Abner Doubleday wanted this game played.

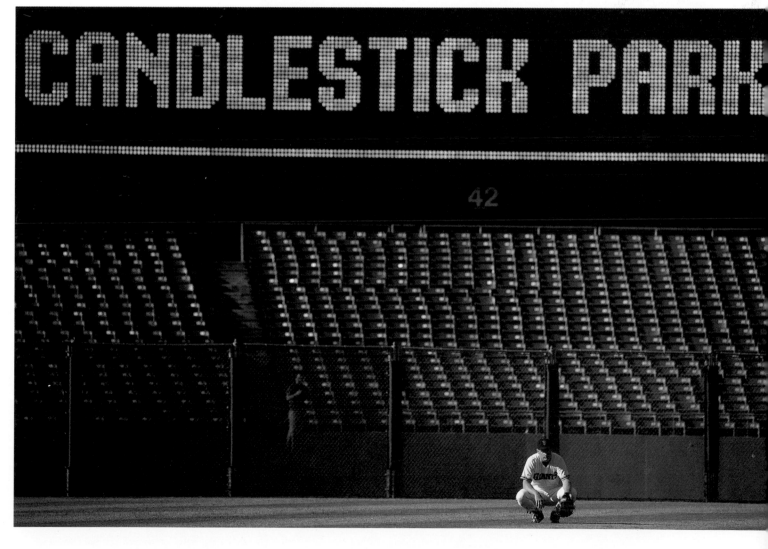

WITNESS TIDY, SYMMETRI-cal, antiseptic Riverfront Stadium in Cincinnati. Or is it Three Rivers Stadium in Pittsburgh? Veteran's Stadium in Philadelphia?

ficial turf, "If a cow can't eat it, I don't want to play on it."

There is no better place to watch a game than Fenway Park or Chicago's Wrigley Field. Not coincidentally, these are the majors' two smallest parks and, as a result, the most intimate. They were built within four years of each other before World War I, when people moved through life at a slower pace. Wrigley has held onto its past more zealously than any other park. To wit, through 1987 there had never been a night baseball game there. This is good, because baseball was meant to be viewed in natural light—try and pick up the rotation on a screwball in the shadows of twilight. Since the advent of night baseball, the neighborhood, fearing rowdy crowds and parking problems, has weathered numerous political battles and studiously avoided the installation of lights. That changed in 1988 when, faced with ownership's overt threats of departure, Chicago's City Council voted to turn on the juice.

Wrigley has two wonderful characteristics found nowhere else: that marvelous, clinging ivy on the brick wall in center field, and the vociferous

"Bleacher Bums." According to the ground rules, the batter gets two bases if the ball gets lost in the vines. The only ground rule in the bleachers is an open disdain for the home team. Oh, the Bleacher Bums love their Cubs. It's just that you'd never know it to hear their running commentary, which tends toward the sarcastic end of the spectrum.

Fenway Park, where Jim Rice hears some of the boos Carl Yastrzemski and Ted Williams used to endure, is a gem. The hulking, green left-field wall made of tin is a national treasure, and the scoreboard that resides within is operated by hand. Fenway is a hitters' park not only for the short porch in right, but because the 33,583 seats don't allow much room for foul territory. Balls that are caught in most stadiums are souvenirs here. Yankee Stadium, which has a shrine to the team's former greats just over the left-field wall, is another place with character. When Los Angelenos begin to feel trapped in the big city, they head for Chavez Ravine and Dodger Stadium, a gorgeous setting for a game. Tiger Stadium in Detroit is one of the league's best parks for both spectators

and batters. Still, not all of the all-natural baseball-only stadiums are perfect. San Francisco's Candlestick Park can be a nasty place to watch a game in April or May—over the course of a day game, fashion in the bleachers can turn from no-shirt chic to parka panache. Meanwhile, pitchers have toiled at Arlington Stadium in Texas amid 106-degree heat. Even baseball loses its appeal at that temperature.

The efficient, sensible (read nefarious), multi-purpose stadiums grew out of the turbulent 1960s. Brilliant city planners, realizing they could display two different sports teams in one stadium, began erecting structures that generally looked like flying saucers—and specifically looked like one another. Atlanta's Fulton County Stadium, home of the Braves and football's Falcons, was the first of the wave in April 1966. Busch Stadium in St. Louis, which offered two breeds of Cardinals, opened a month later. Those facilities were followed, in order, by Cincinnati, Pittsburgh, and Philadelphia. Or was that Philadelphia, Pittsburgh, and Cincinnati? With the exception of Atlanta, those cities laid artificial turf on the floor rather than natural sod. This enabled players like Pete Rose to dribble a baseball in basketball fashion. Imagine the effect on knees. Oh, the horror.

"I hate the turf," says Willie Randolph, the Yankee's all-star second baseman. "It shouldn't be in the game. Period. When they went to artificial turf, you couldn't compare baseball's different eras any more. That's part of baseball, arguing who's better. Well, today the turf takes away the bad bounces, and it turns singles into doubles and triples. When I think about baseball as a kid, it was pure. Maybe I'm old-fashioned, but it's an old-fashioned game. It was meant to be played on grass and dirt."

These double-decked wonders with artificial additives are distinguished by their good supply of bad seats. Was there a connection between the wan-

ing popularity of ant farms in the 1970s and the emergence of multi-purpose stadiums?

The next logical progression was domed stadiums. The Astrodome, the self proclaimed "Eighth Wonder of the World," was actually in business in 1965, but it took a while for the phenomenon to catch on. True, there were no longer rainouts, but the price extracted was great: The air-conditioning is favorable to left-handed hitters, balls that are hit off the roof or speakers and land in fair territory are fair game, no grass where the sun doesn't shine. This is where AstroTurf was first used. The Minnesota Twins play in the Hubert H. Humphrey Metrodome, fondly known as the Homerdome because baseballs fly over the surreal plastic fences—the players call them garbage bags—with alarming

regularity. The 50-ton canvas roof at Olympic Stadium in Montreal is supported by a 55-story mast. The saving grace here is a $1 bleacher ticket.

Because teams play half their games at home, they are built to exploit the local surroundings. Thus, the St. Louis Cardinals are fleet-footed, line-drive hitters who can hit the gaps in the springy outfield and run down those balls when they're playing defense. The Yankees are traditionally long on hitting and short on pitching; with that cavernous left field, who needs pitching? In Boston, the Red Sox are always looking for a right-handed hitter with a short, efficient uppercut. Left-handed pitchers generally fare miserably at Fenway. The Tigers always seem to have a slugger or two who can stroke the long ball. Home, after all, is where the hits are.

The Baseball

It just begs to be thrown or hit, this five-ounce sphere that is nine centimeters in circumference. Yet, its fits-perfectly-in-the-hand design is deceptively complex.

The center is cushion-cork, wrapped in a small layer of rubber. Next, there's a six-ply gray yarn that is 80 percent virgin wool, followed by four-ply white yarn (75 percent wool), three-ply gray yarn (80 percent wool), five-ply white cotton thread, and another layer of synthetic thread. The ball is wrapped by machine in places like Taiwan, Haiti, and Korea, then the leather cover is sewn in place by hand with exactly eighty-eight stitches. From 1876 to 1976, Spalding supplied baseballs to the major leagues. But when the practice ceased to be cost-effective, Rawlings took on the chore. Today, Rawlings produces about half of the world's annual twelve million baseballs.

For such an innocent object, the baseball generates its share of controversy. Since the time of Babe Ruth, the ball's liveliness has been debated. In 1920, Ruth hit fifty-four home runs in his first season with the New York Yankees, touching off the era of the lively ball. Then in the late 1960s, the dead-ball era, pitchers began to dominate. Detroit's Denny McLain won 31 games in 1968, the same year seven pitchers produced earned-run averages of less than 2.00. In 1970, however, Tom Seaver was the only National League pitcher with an ERA lower than 3.00. Home run production began to increase, and players said the ball had been juiced up. Major league baseball officials deny this, of course.

Pitchers began to develop the upper hand again in the early 1980s; then, oddly enough, baseballs began flying out of parks again. In 1986, major leaguers hit a record 3,813 home runs. A year later, an incredible 4,458 home runs were recorded. Detroit Tigers manager Sparky Anderson called it "the nitro ball." Pitchers called it names you'll have to imagine.

"We played a game at Yankee Stadium," says pitcher John Candelaria, then with the Angels, "and Jack Howell shattered his bat with this one pitch—and it went ten rows into the seats. He's a strong kid, but I don't know if he's that strong."

There is a technical term for the "liveliness" of a baseball, known as the *coefficient of restitution*. The

COR is basically the ball's energy. This is measured by directing a ball toward a steel plate at the speed of 88 feet per second, roughly the speed of a pitched ball. The energy retained by the ball as it rebounds off the steel is the COR. The major league's specifications require that a ball's COR be between .53 and .57; that means the ball must retain between 53 and 57 percent of its energy or speed. Players conducted their own tests in 1987, comparing the bounce produced by new and old balls. Theories abound.

Pitchers (and even a few hitters) maintain that baseball's brain trust has added oomph to the ball by altering its construction. Though there is no way to prove these allegations, there seems to be a connection between home runs and public interest.

When the home run record was set in 1986, some 47 million fans came out to the park. That all-time mark was broken a year later, as more than 52 million people attended games. Some players offer the Happy Haitian Theory. When President Jean-Claude (Baby Doc) Duvalier fled Haiti in early 1986, a player explains, his face broadening into a smile, the country's population was greatly relieved to be out from under the 28-year dictatorship that began with his father, François (Papa Doc). Thus the laborers were happier and, in their new zeal, wound the baseballs tighter. Makes a sort of bizarre sense, doesn't it? A Rawlings competitor who shall remain nameless speculates that the escalating price of leather is the culprit. By shaving the leather cover thinner to save money, the ball becomes smaller and therefore flies farther.

Baseballs would never work their way into play if it wasn't for Burns Bintliff. For fifty years now this Millsboro, Delaware, man has been supplying the major leagues with, well, mud. It's called Lena Blackburne's Baseball Rubbing Mud, and every ball that winds up in a pitcher's hand gets rubbed down with a healthy dose. The mud, a special blend developed by a Philadelphia Athletics third-base coach around 1930, takes the shine off the cowhide and allows pitchers to get a grip on it. This special blend from the Delaware River arrives each spring at major-league offices in an anonymous silver coffee can. Maybe that's the secret of the newly hyperactive baseball; the caffeine simply rubs off.

The Uniform

The New York Yankees and New York Mets, as befits the financial capital of the world, go to work each day in pinstripes. Three major-league teams—the Baltimore Orioles, St. Louis Cardinals, and Toronto Blue Jays—are for the, uh, birds. There are no Lions in baseball, but Tigers and young bears (Cubs) reside in Detroit and Chicago. Indians can be found in Cleveland; Atlanta is the home of the Braves. For some reason, teams in Boston (Red) and Chicago (White) are named for socks, though the peculiar spelling is Sox, and, technically, the Bostonians don't wear red socks at all—they wear fancy white hose. The high seas are represented by Pittsburgh's Pirates and the more modern Mariners of Seattle. There are Angels in California, though the conversations in the dugout at Anaheim Stadium are hardly celestial. And how about those men of the pinstriped cloth in San Diego, the Padres?

Local references are quite big in the majors: Who can deny the appeal of the Texas Rangers, the Minnesota Twins, the Montreal Expos, or the Milwaukee Brewers? On the other hand, what genius can be blamed for coming up with the redundant and

SOME PLAYERS BEND THE rules and wear their stirrups high, while others make their fashion statement with accessories. Call it uniform chic.

repetitious Philadelphia Phillies?

As you might imagine, the uniforms run the gamut. Admittedly, there is only so much you can do with a cap and polyester togs, which explains why there are a few good-looking uniforms and a few more that belong on softball diamonds.

The Yankees do not have the patent rights to pinstripes, but those narrow navy blue stripes are unmistakably New York. The simple, superimposed "NY" gives the Yankees baseball's classiest uniforms. New York outfielder Dave Winfield, an admitted traditionalist, says, "It's a good-looking uniform, and I look good in it." At six-foot-six, 220 pounds, go ahead and argue with him. The breathlessly patriotic red, white, and blue Yankees

insignia, depicting Uncle Sam's star-spangled hat atop a Louisville Slugger, thankfully appears nowhere on the uniform.

The Tigers have a fairly silly logo—the catatonic cat appears to have been struck by an errant line drive—but the grand Old English "D" more than compensates. Detroit wears white uniforms with navy blue piping at home and grey on the road. The Braves have a uniform that belongs to the era of *The Natural:* white trimmed in scarlet and navy with the word Braves written in script, slanting upward from left to right. The shirt—and this is essential for the old-time flavor—is a button-down number, as opposed to the horrid pullovers worn by the Cincinnati Reds, Chicago Cubs, and New

York Mets, among many others. Cleveland has fairly typical uniforms, but the smiling presence of Chief Wahoo (that's his real name) sets the Indians apart. The Cardinals, perhaps because they are from the staid National League, go for realism on their uniform: Two redbirds sit perched on a gold bat. The Baltimore Orioles, those fun-loving American Leaguers, employ a feisty cartoon character swinging a bat bigger than he is. Toronto, in an effort to get everything in, offers a faithful rendition of a blue jay over the image of a baseball with a traditional maple leaf inset nicely.

Okay, so maybe pinstripes were taken—the Twins, Cubs, Mets, Phillies, and Padres had appropriated the design anyway—but surely the Houston Astros could have come up with something better than those burnt-orange disasters they insisted on wearing for years. The Astros may fashion themselves as stars, as their uniform suggests, but fashion plates they aren't. The new, understated uniform still has a grating effect.

For a long while, no one was quite sure what that red, white, and blue agglomeration was that the Montreal Expos carried around on their caps and shirts. Hubie Brooks, one of the Expos most popular players, explains that the whole thing is supposed to be a large "M" with a lowercase "e" and "b" tucked into the flourishes, standing for Expos and baseball. "Don't feel bad," Brooks says. "It took me two years to figure it out." Some people think the "e" is actually a "c" and therefore a clever tribute to owner Charles Bronfman. Maybe. The Milwaukee logo might have been designed during a tour of one of the city's great breweries: The M and the B are fashioned somewhat in the shape of a hideous mauve mitt.

Thanks to a happy accident of timing, sometimes bad can be good. Take the Oakland Athletics of the 1970s. They won three consecutive World Se-

ries from 1972 to 1974, and they did it in obnoxious Kelly green and Fort Knox gold uniforms designed by owner Charlie Finley himself. While Haight-Ashbury, with its psychedelic purple doors, hummed in a far-out universe of its own across the Bay, the A's had their own thing going on in Oakland. They wore long hair and moustaches, and their garish uniforms perfectly summed up the flower-power generation. "They laughed at us a lot," says former Oakland pitcher Catfish Hunter, "but we got used to it after a while. The only break we got was on Sunday—that was when we wore virgin white with green and gold trim." Now, of course, Oakland's uniforms, though recently streamlined, are anachronistic and just a little bit ugly.

Blatant ridicule keeps major-league fashion on a fairly conservative level. The Phillies experimented with zippers on their shirts for a while, but changed back to buttons in 1987. Some years ago, the Chicago White Sox decided they would rather look like milkmen than ballplayers. Much to the chagrin of the players, the Chisox actually wore shorts. After unanimously bad reviews, the team mercifully changed back to a more conventional look.

There isn't a lot of room for individualism when all twenty-five players have to suit up in the same uniform, but there are small windows for style. The stirrups that are worn outside the sanitary socks can be lengthened for the long, lean look. Batting gloves are in vogue—some players even have a special pair for base running. Lately, players have become walking billboards for athletic companies. Shoes are a matter of personal taste (and the size of the contract a player can extract). There are gaudy sweatbands, not to mention leather gloves with a black or blue hue. As far as baseball experts have determined, there is no connection between looking good and playing well. It's a good thing, too.

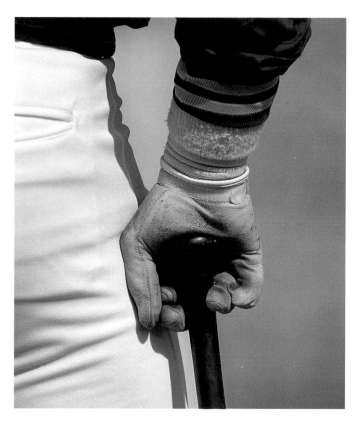

CAPS ARE THE PLAYER'S
most versatile piece of clothing (left).
They look good with gloves, close to
the heart, even askew.

NO VISITORS ALLOWED. IN the clubhouse (left), a player can work on his swing in peace, while the dugout (below) offers freedom of choice, whether it's to blow bubbles or chew tobacco.

The Inner Sanctums

Roger McDowell, the New York Mets' off-center reliever, is sitting on the stool at his locker in the team's clubhouse. Clad only in his underwear, McDowell is shoveling the last few chunks of pineapple off his plate and into his mouth. Though he's talking to a complete stranger, McDowell is un-questionably relaxed.

"This is great," he says, waving around the room. "I enjoy coming to the park. A lot of people, with the fields they're in, hate going to work. Not me. Hey, it's got nothing to do with the money I'm making. You get free food, gum, and stuff. They do your laundry, shine your shoes. I like the atmosphere. In here, it's like family. You can talk about anything. You know the old clubhouse saying, 'What you see here, what you say here, what you hear here—let it stay here when you leave here.' It's true. This is our own little world."

The clubhouse, the dugout, the bullpen—these are the inner sanctums where baseball players get away from the rest of the world, where boys are quite simply boys. This is where marital problems are discussed, good restaurants are discovered, soap operas are dissected. Players arrive for a night game as early as two p.m. and often don't leave until ten hours later. During the season, they spend more time here than anyplace else. As McDowell notes, players enjoy all the comforts. Uniforms, from shirts to spikes, are laid out by the clubhouse men. Food is spread out buffet-style—everything from artery-clogging fried chicken to fresh veggies. All the small neccessities of this game aren't far away. There is a wide variety of tobacco, gum, and sunflower seeds for the player who insists on chewing. In a quiet corner, a card game can usually be found in session. The newspapers are digested, along with a cup of coffee. Beer, generally, is the beverage of choice after a game.

Baseball is spoken here. More than athletes in any other sport, baseball players contribute to the oral tradition by trading anecdotes. A player will suddenly leap off his stool and assume the batter's position to underline a point. In this private place, humor is the universal language. Players are still giving each other the old hotfoot routine, the atomic-balm-in-the-jock trick. There are elaborate constructions—Phil and Joe Niekro like to send their police friends into visiting clubhouses to arrest people—and the simple pyrotechnics of pitcher Dave Stieb, who upon his demotion from the starting rotation set his shoes on fire. Some insensitive players have been known to decorate cakes and pies from the adoring public with the bare resources at hand.

The trainer's room is the last frontier; even baseball writers aren't allowed. This is where unfortunate players hide from the media after

WITH THE DODGERS UP 9–2 in the ninth, the Mets' bullpen is a place where a middle reliever suffers in silence.

surrendering the home run that lost the game. Though the dugout and bullpens are more open to public scrutiny, players are still themselves there. During their stretch drive in 1986, a group of Mets, including McDowell, Ron Darling, Howard Johnson, and Bob Ojeda, took to wearing an odd assortment of "rally caps." This headgear, fashioned from towels and caps, was designed to bring New York luck. When they won the World Series no one was laughing. The New York Yankees still remember pitcher Ron Guidry's target practice a few years back. Yankee manager Billy Martin, a worrywart in the dugout, had the nervous habit of pacing back and forth. Guidry, who is only slightly more accurate with a baseball than a stream of tobacco juice, tried to see how close he could come to Martin's shoes each time the manager scurried by. Pretty close. After a few innings, the whole bench was giggling.

The exiled pitchers and catchers out in the bullpen have ample opportunity to survey the talent in the stands. Not all games, after all, are of the scintillating variety. All these diversions merely help fill in the gaps between long innings. As McDowell says, "Even the greatest jobs can get a little slow at times."

Laborers in the Field

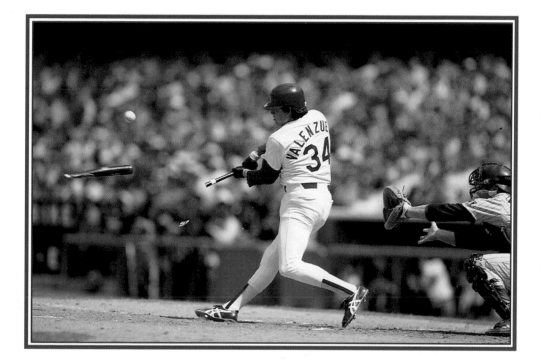

The Pitcher

On the surface, this is not such a bad job. Go out every fourth or fifth day, play catch with the fellow behind the plate for two or three hours, take a shower, and go home. The perks are outstanding: A healthy annual salary that can exceed $1 million, thousands of admiring fans, frequent-flier miles, the opportunity to get a terrific suntan.

Over the years, however, the pitcher has been a persecuted breed. Perhaps everyone in management is merely jealous of their situation. Maybe they're just too good. Depending on who you talk to, pitching is the essence of baseball: Some people suggest it is 70 percent of the game. It could be 90.

"I've heard all those numbers," says John Candelaria, a left-hander who gave his best years to the Pittsburgh Pirates in the 1970s. "All I know is, I've got the ball on the mound and the hitter can't do anything with it until I say so. You'd have to say the pitcher has the upper hand."

How else to explain the uneven Boston Red Sox, who perennially have one of the major leagues' best-hitting teams? In 1967, Boston led all teams with 722 runs and 158 home runs and ultimately reached the World Series, despite a shortage of top-line pitching talent. The National League entry, the St. Louis Cardinals, had averaged one less run per game over the regular season, but had superb pitching. The

Redbirds' earned run average of 3.05 held up in the World Series as Boston was permitted to score only 21 runs in seven games. St. Louis won because it was able to pummel Red Sox pitching for 25 runs. In 1946, Boston led the majors in runs, doubles, and batting average; the Cardinals had the best ERA. Naturally, St. Louis beat Boston in the Series in seven games. Even today, the two teams carry on in their particular traditions. Pitching-poor Boston has been to the Series four times since beating Chicago in 1918 and lost every time. The Cardinals still have anemic bats, but great pitching helps explain why they've been to fifteen World Series over that span and won eight times.

THE METS' DWIGHT GOODEN (left), a.k.a. Dr. K, is one of baseball's most dominant pitchers. Not only is his fastball a ninety-mile-an-hour flick of the serpent's tongue, but his curveball, when it's tight, is unhittable. Chicago's Rick Sutcliffe (below) isn't as overpowering, but is often just as effective.

Good pitching always keeps you in the game. It doesn't take a nuclear physicist to explain the relationship between an opponent's runs scored and success or failure. With a low score, as managers like to say to the point of fatigue, there is always a chance to win the contest. Ask a manager which he'd rather have—a great slugger or a consistent stopper—and he won't even hesitate. Why?

Even in the best circumstances, the hitter will only reach the plate five or six times in a game. The pitcher, on the other hand, is on the mound for half the game and is responsible for recording twenty-seven outs. Not only does he have eight teammates helping him, but he often knows something the hitter doesn't: Where the ball is going and how it will get there. Contrary to conventional baseball thinking, the pitcher is the aggressor, the offense. Though this doesn't always work out on the diamond, in theory the pitcher and the catcher choose a pitch and location, say a fastball on the outside corner of the plate. The hitter, who may still be thinking about the curveball that broke too close inside or the weak change-up that got him off-stride, can only speculate. He is placed in a reactionary situation. Even if he gets his bat on the ball that comes steaming in from only sixty feet away, the fielders, who know how their team is attacking the hitter, are usually placed in the optimum position to collect his offerings.

This is an intellectual enterprise, which explains why there is a place for those craftsmen whose fastball maxes out at a mere 85 miles an hour next to the fireballers. Good pitchers know that sometimes making them hit the ball is more important than making them miss. Sandy Koufax and Nolan Ryan come to mind. Ryan is the prototypical power pitcher, a thrower. Through 1987, he had struck out an all-time record 4,547 batters with a fastball that was once clocked at 100.8

THE PITCHER IS THE MAN IN control. He holds the ball until he's ready to throw—but once it's gone, he's at the mercy of the hitter.

miles an hour. Nobody has ever thrown it harder. Still, Ryan didn't always know where it was going. In eight seasons with the California Angels, Ryan led the American League seven times in strikeouts. For six of those years, he also led the league in walks; this explains Ryan's career record, which hovers below .500. Koufax didn't have Ryan's speed—these days, baseball people call it velocity—but his fastball smoked right along and his curve was positively lethal. The difference was control. The year he struck out 382 batters to lead the majors, 1965, Koufax walked exactly 71. As his left elbow gave way to arthritis, Koufax learned even more about the art of pitching. He was 53–17 over his last two seasons before retiring at the age of thirty-one.

Don Sutton has never blinded people, but he knows how to keep hitters off balance. Location, not speed, is his specialty. That explains his aversion to the radar guns that have changed the way scouts look at prospects. "If I were to show 87 or 88, I'd wonder because the guy operating it must be on something," Sutton says. "I'd have to take a urine test. As long as it registers, I'm not concerned. But if I see a guy banging on the back of it because he's not getting a reading, I'll worry." Sutton, for the record, has won 321 games during his career, one of history's best totals.

The pitcher's preeminence over the years has led to all kinds of drastic measures to ensure fair play. The athletes themselves take this personally. Back in 1920, the ball was made much livelier to accommodate a young slugger named Babe Ruth. In 1969, the pitching mound was lowered from 15 to 10 inches. This effectively took away some of the pitcher's leverage. Beginning in the 1970s, baseballs

PITCHERS DO NOT COME IN A STANDARD SIZE or shape. The Angels' Mike Witt (far left) is 6-foot-7, 185 pounds; Fernando Valenzuela of the Dodgers (left) is eight inches shorter but weighs the same. The Yankees' Tommy John (below), he of the bionic elbow, is still at work as he approaches age fifty.

started jumping out of ball parks again. Pitchers have a conspiracy theory: Management, believing (mistakenly) that spectators would rather see a 7–5 game than a 2–0 contest, secretly called for livelier baseballs to give the hitters another unfair advantage. "It's always something," Candelaria says. "But if you can't deal with it, go find another job. It's like life; if you don't adjust, it'll go by you. That's what pitching is: making adjustments." Umpires are part of the scheme, too. They have taken an increasingly dim view of the pitcher's chief ally, the brushback pitch, and it is they who are responsible for the incredible shrinking strike zone. Technically, the strike zone is the area over the plate between a batter's knees and letters. Through time the zone has moved down from the letters to the belt, costing pitchers at least a cubic foot of valuable air space. Before the 1988 season, partially in response to the raft of home runs the year before, baseball's powers announced that the full strike zone—from the knees to the belt—would be enforced.

Pitchers will believe it when they see it.

The Hitter

LOOK AT THIS FACE: HOW could Wade Boggs not be a hitter? The ability to filter out all the distractions that come with the game is his hallmark. That explains Boggs' career batting average of .350-plus.

"It's a round bat and a round ball," the third-base coach says, offering one of baseball's profoundest clichés. "You've got to hit it square."

It is harder than it sounds, and when the hitter digs in at the plate, he battles some amazing odds. First of all, there are usually thousands of people watching him, and not all of them are sitting on their hands. There could be wind or rain or an April chill—enemies all of the batter's fragile concentration. If twilight has graced the field or the players are working under unnatural light, hitting becomes more difficult. The bad guy, the pitcher, towers on the mound a mere 60 feet away, grinning mischievously at his catcher. He is in control here. A fastball under the chin? Perhaps a breaking ball away? Or an off-speed pitch in the dirt? The hitter can only guess. Whatever the offering, it will roll in somewhere between 80 and 90 miles an hour, which means the batter has about half a second to decide whether or not he wants to try to hit it. If so, he must start the bat head through the strike zone even as the pitcher is releasing the ball. If he is lucky, the hitter will correctly adjust his swing to meet the ball and the bat (whose diameter cannot exceed 2.75 inches) will strike the ball (2.87 inches around) within a quarter of an inch of its center. Provided the hitter has timed his swing properly, the ball will return to the field of play between first and third base. Now, if it somehow manages to elude the pitcher and his four infielders and fall to earth before any of the three outfielders can snag it, the hitter has succeeded. It is a lot to hope for.

According to the *Baseball Encyclopedia,* Ty Cobb had the highest all-time career batting average, .367 over

24 seasons. The Georgia Peach never had to deal with night baseball or relief specialists, but his accomplishment is telling. Cobb failed in his mission at the plate more than 63 percent of the time. Pete Rose, who broke Cobb's record for hits (4,191) in 1985, finished his career with a .303 average, which means pitchers were .697 against him.

The great hitters espouse different theories and techniques—this truly is a weird science—but they have several things in common: superb eyesight, terrific hand-eye coordination, a thorough knowledge of the strike zone, and, for the most part, uncommon patience. It doesn't hurt to be left-handed, either. When it all works together, the ball seems to float in bigger than a balloon. The three best hitters of this present era (solely for average) are Don Mattingly of the New York

Yankees, the San Diego Padres' Tony Gwynn, and Wade Boggs of the Boston Red Sox. Listen to Gwynn:

"I sat down with [Mattingly] at a batting clinic and that's when I saw it. He just doesn't get excited. He's calm, it's like he's under control all the time. That's why he's such a good hitter. It seems like he's so nonchalant, like he's not even trying. Guys like him and Wade Boggs, they make it look so easy."

But of course it isn't. All the raw ingredients of talent mean nothing if a player isn't willing to work hard in the care and feeding of his swing. Mattingly and Boggs are obsessed with this, which might explain their career batting averages of .331 and .354, respectively, through 1987. And while both Midwest-born left-handers broke into professional baseball in 1982 as largely overlooked draft choices and

their careers have traced parallel curves, Mattingly and Boggs have come to different conclusions about where their value to their teams lies.

"I try to pull the ball more than he does," Mattingly says. "When I came up, I hit just like he did—you know, going with pitches to left and left-center. Now, I try to get the bat out front more. I'm trying to produce more runs." In 1984, Mattingly won the American League batting title with a .343 average. A season later, Mattingly produced 217 runs (runs scored, plus runs batted in, minus home runs), the most by a Yankee since Joe DiMaggio's 1948 season. In 1987, Mattingly tied a major-league record by hitting home runs in eight consecutive games.

Boggs guesses he could hit more than 30 home runs a year, but chooses a more cautious route. "I'm just trying to get on base," he says. "With our

team, that's my job. If it takes a walk, fine. If it means taking a pitch the other way, fine." Boggs' 240 hits in 1985 were the most in the majors since 1930. Factor in his 96 walks that season and it totals a fairly incredible on-base percentage of .450, a figure that led both leagues by far.

While Mattingly constantly experiments with his swing, and tinkers with the mechanics, Boggs' secret to consistency is repetition. Boggs' routine in Boston never, ever, deviates from the following: At three p.m. he leaves his apartment for Fenway Park. At three-thirty he sits in front of his locker and changes into his uniform. He walks to the dugout at four p.m. and warms up his arm ten minutes later. At four-fifteen, Boggs takes grounders at third base for twenty to twenty-five minutes. Then he steps on third base, second base, and first

base—always in that order—before retiring to the dugout.

Boggs learned about time from his father, a former Marine and Air Force man. "Dinner was always at five-thirty, and if you weren't home at five-thirty, you didn't eat," Boggs says. "So you learned to always know where the clocks were in your friends' houses, and to this day I always notice clocks. I woke up at precisely the same time every day for eighteen years. If I woke up, say, thirty minutes late, I was out of sync all day."

It gets much worse, too. Boggs, as the poultry people love to point out, eats chicken every day. Honestly, every day. His wife, Karen, eventually wrote a cookbook, *Foul Tips,* out of self-defense. Truly, when Boggs steps up to the dinner plate, like all great hitters, he gets comfortable, protects the plate, and starts going to work.

THE YANKEES' DON MATtingly (far left) and the San Diego Padres' Tony Gwynn (above) are cut from the same cloth as Wade Boggs. They both have style, consistency, and patience at the plate.

The Slugger

*TWO VERY DIFFERENT SLUG-
gers: (left) Reggie Jackson was
willing to look bad in pursuit of a
homer, while the Yankees' Dave
Winfield (below) got a piece of the
ball more often.*

slugger *n. [Colloq.] a person
who slugs; specifically, a) a
prizefighter who punches hard,
b) a baseball player with a high
percentage of extra-base hits.*

Close your eyes and imagine the prototypical baseball slugger. He has rippling forearms, hulking shoulders, and a good sense of timing for a large fellow. He's a club's meal ticket who, with one swing of the bat from his cleanup position, can compensate for otherwise anemic hitting, bad pitching, or indifferent fielding. The slugger, like his boxing counterpart, hits hard and doesn't mind missing once in a while. This is the all-or-nothing essence of the slugger.

Babe Ruth, whose nickname "The Sultan of Swat" just reeked of unbridled power, is the all-time slugging leader with a .690 percentage. The figure, which represents the number of total bases divided by at-bats, far outdistances Ted Williams' second-place mark of .634. Ruth hit 714 home runs, which means he hit one out roughly every twelfth at-bat. In ten World Series appearances, Ruth hit fifteen home runs in 129 at-bats, the best ratio ever. And because Ruth was such a complete hitter, he didn't miss as often as you might expect. Ruth struck out only 1,330 times in 8,399 at-bats. Hank Aaron, the only man to hit more homers than Ruth (755), was remarkable in that respect. He came to the plate 12,364 times and struck out only 1,383 times.

Many modern-day sluggers are something less than the genuine article; they have tunnel vision when it comes to home runs. Take Reggie Jackson. His 563 career home runs are sixth on the all-time list, but his 2,597 strike-outs are an embarrassing major-league

record. That means Jackson suffered more than four strikeouts for every homer, or twice as many as Ruth and Aaron. He'll take them. Jackson would do anything to hit a home run, up to and including taking a seat in the dirt after a wild swing. Like many sluggers, Jackson thrived on big moments. In the 1977 World Series against the Los Angeles Dodgers, Jackson hit three homers in three swings for the New York Yankees. Dave Kingman never had the opportunity to play in a World Series, but he was in Jackson's class. Though Kingman hit 442 career home runs, he struck out 1,866 times in 6,677 career at-bats. Thus, Kingman's strikeout ratio of .279 was higher than his batting average of .236.

Like Jackson and Kingman, Ruth was an imposing man. His six-foot-two, 215-pound frame was partially responsible for those startling numbers. Clearly, there is a correlation betwen size and slugging percentage. The best five sluggers in history—Ruth, Williams, Lou Gehrig, Jimmie Foxx, and Hank Greenberg—averaged six-foot-two, 205 pounds. Rogers Hornsby and Willie Mays are the only two players in the all-time top ten who stood shorter than six feet tall. Hornsby's career batting average (.358) is history's second best and, for a 170-pounder, Mays' strength was unworldly. Like the great sluggers, they knew how to throw their weight around when it mattered most.

Today's sluggers are a diverse lot. There is twelve-year veteran Jack Clark, who in 1987 hit 35 home runs and drove in 106 runs in only 131 games. Clark is paid handsomely—roughly $1.5 million a season—to clear the bases, though his health has been an Achilles' heel over the years. In 1988, Clark left the St. Louis Cardinals, where he was the only potent bat in the lineup, for a stint with the New York Yankees. And with the Yankees' brutal batting order, opposing pitchers weren't as likely to pitch around Clark, a delightful thought.

"I've always been the type of player who just comes out there, takes my chances, and swings the bat," Clark says. "I'm a slugger and I like to see a few decent pitches." Clark's definition of a true slugger? "He isn't just a home-run hitter. He's a guy who is a threat to hit a home run, but can get that run home any way he has to." Oakland rookie Mark McGwire hit 49 home runs in 1987; if early reviews mean anything, he may be one of those modern sluggers. Perhaps following in the footsteps of Jackson, McGwire went down swinging 131 times in the process.

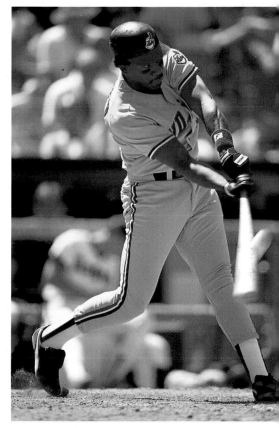

MARK McGWIRE OF THE OAK-land A's hit forty-nine home runs in 1987—and he also struck out 131 times. Darryl Strawberry of the New York Mets (left) and Joe Carter of the Cleveland Indians (above) are also sluggers of the modern era.

The Outfielder

The outfield is where the good hitters stand when they can't be at the plate. Yes, it's almost as dull and commonplace as it sounds, a necessary evil. Shagging flies, or someone else's mistakes, can be a positively annoying experience, but it's the price you pay for those four or five at-bats each game. Former catcher Tim McCarver sums it up: "I would say probably most outfielders who were elected to the Hall of Fame were predominantly number-four hitters."

In other words, their value lies in swinging a bat, rather than slinging a leather glove. This is a generalization—there have been some marvelous defensive outfielders—but it underlines the approach most players take toward playing the outfield. "There are times," says the New York Yankees' Dave Winfield, "when it drags a little out there."

Thus, the most important asset for an outfielder, beyond a healthy bat, is concentration. It's really that simple. The good ones stay interested; the vacant ones, perhaps still trying to fathom the ungodly slider that struck them out, get caught once in awhile. Pete Rose's 4,256 hits are a major-league record, but his intensity can be better seen in his fielding percentage of .991 in the outfield, a figure matched by only three other players. On balance, it is less critical for out-

THE OUTFIELDER IS THE
last line of defense. If the ball gets
by him, the game could be over be-
fore it's over.

THERE IS NO REPLACEMENT for speed in the outfield. The Cardinals have some of baseball's fleetest feet, including Willie McGee who hauls in a would-be double.

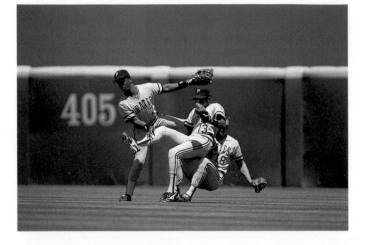

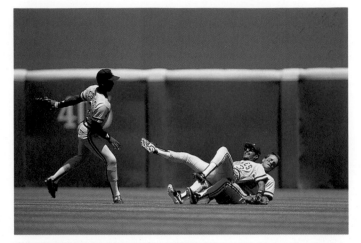

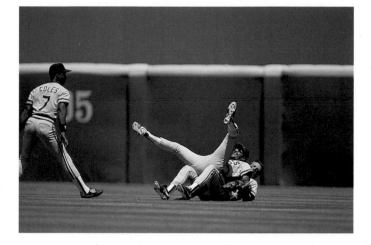

fielders to stay wired into a game, since they see fewer chances. Still, the stakes are high: When they make a mistake it can cost two or three bases; the penalty for an infielder's gaffe is usually a single base.

Hubie Brooks of the Montreal Expos has played both sides of the fence. He started out in junior college as a center fielder and continued in the outfield through Triple-A ball. The New York Mets saw him as a third baseman or a shortstop. After he was traded to Montreal, the Expos decided his hitting would improve if he was shifted back to the outfield. "You need less concentration out there," Brooks says. "In the infield, you're ninety feet from the ball on every pitch, you've got to be ready, know where you're going with the ball, and make a perfect throw every time. In the outfield, you relax a little more. You've got more time to react. The whole trick is getting a jump on the ball."

Easier said than executed. The good outfielders know the tendencies of the hitters, and cheat accordingly. If the left-handed batter likes to go with the pitch to the opposite field, the left fielder will shade the line. The weaker the hitter, the closer the center fielder creeps. And so on. Once positioned, instinct and speed play a huge factor in an outfielder's success. Fielding percentages don't always reflect the value of a team's outfield, because

errors can't be made on balls which can't be reached. Richie Ashburn, of Philadelphia, reached a lot of balls other outfielders couldn't. Between 1951 and 1958, Ashburn had six of the ten best all-time seasons in terms of putouts. Today's fleet outfielders (St. Louis, Montreal, and Toronto usually have terrific team speed) routinely turn doubles into singles and triples into outs.

The most sensitive position is center field, because there is so much ground to cover. Every ball that comes that way is in play; there are no foul lines to protect the center fielder. Consequently, he is generally the fastest man on the field. Willie Mays made some famous catches, but most people don't realize he ran down more outfield flies (7,095) than any man in history. Center field is so important from a defensive standpoint that a manager will accept a tradeoff; long-time Baltimore Oriole Paul Blair hit an even .250 in seventeen years, but he was one of the finest center fielders ever to play the game.

Because of the distance from home plate and third base, the key to success as a right fielder is to have a strong arm. If first base is already taken, left field is where the defensive liabilities are often stationed. Even when those players are reeling in someone's line drive, they're wishing they were on the other end of it.

AS THE PITTSBURGH PI-rates demonstrate (top, left to right), the outfield isn't always just a place to work on your tan. Meanwhile, Kevin Bass of the Astros (left) hauls one in at the wall.

The Infielder

For years, the infielder has been a second-class citizen, a hard-working caddy for high-paid pitchers and outfielders. That all changed in 1988, when a five-foot-ten, 155-pound sprite named Osborne Earl Smith earned a salary of $2.3 million. This made him not only the highest-paid shortstop of all time, but the highest-paid *player* ever. Ozzie Smith, the Wizard of Oz, brought new respect to infielders with breathtaking plays for the St. Louis Cardinals. Just ask Dan Gladden of the Minnesota Twins.

Hang time is a term associated with basketball, but in game six of the 1987 World Series, Smith did something baseball people hadn't seen before. Gladden, the Twins' fastest runner, hit a chopper to deep short, and Smith hesitated for a brief second. If he had waited for the ball to come down, he wouldn't have had a chance at getting Gladden out at first, so Smith charged and leaped and met the ball at its apex, took it from his glove, spun, and made the throw to first—all in midair. Gladden was safe, but those who saw

A PROTOTYPICAL FIRST baseman, Keith Hernandez (above) thinks he has picked off the Cubs' Davey Lopes, although the umpire begs to differ. (right) The Wizard of Oz turns two on Cincinnati.

THE INFIELDER DOESN'T always get his man, but he can look awfully good trying. The Yankees' Mike Pagliarulo (right) missed this ball, even with a boost from the California Angels.

the play will never forget it. There have been dozens of similarly impossible plays from Smith, a dazzling performer sometimes given to taking his position before the game via a backflip. In 1980, he reached more balls (621) than any shortstop in history. Through 1987, Smith had won eight Gold Gloves, a testimony to his fielding excellence, and maintained a field-

ing percentage that hovered around a staggering .980, on a par with the all-time marks established by Larry Bowa and Mark Belanger.

Smith aside, sometimes infielders are the only ones who can appreciate other infielders' contributions. "Nobody much notices us," says New York Yankees second baseman Willie Randolph, "until we screw up. But we're in the game on every pitch, ready to make something happen." Presumably something good.

Just as infielders can make a pitcher's life infinitely easier (or more difficult), a pitcher can return the favor. "The most important thing is to throw strikes for those guys," says Catfish Hunter, who worked on the Oakland mound like a man possessed.

"Don't waste time. If the infielders get too relaxed, if you fool around and they lose interest, they're not going to make the plays for you."

The shortstop, if he is sufficiently into the game, is going to make the most plays for you. After the catcher, he is the most important defensive player on the field because he gets the most chances. Why? Most batters in

THE KEY TO BASEBALL IS
*having your head in the game and
your eye on the ball—but not simultaneously.*

the major leagues are right-handed and try to pull the ball toward left field. Luis Aparicio (2,581 games, 8,016 assists), Rabbit Maranville (5,139 putouts), and Bill Dahlen (13,325 chances) are baseball's most enduring shortstops, according to the record book.

The second baseman, who patrols the turf on the other side of second base, is the other pure infielder. Like shortstops, second basemen aren't particulary known for their batting feats. Jerry Lumpe, whose fielding percentage of .984 is the best ever for a second baseman, hit only .268 for three American League teams in the 1950s and '60s. There have been exceptions—Eddie Collins, Joe Morgan, and Nellie Fox (who appeared in the most games at second) were all pretty fair hitters.

Generally, third base offers the best combination of offensive and defensive athletic skills. Some of today's most versatile performers—Mike Schmidt, Wade Boggs, George Brett—are third basemen. With weak-hitting teammates at short and second, the third baseman must wield a potent bat. He also needs a glove capable of snagging a smash down the line on one hop. That's why they call it the Hot Corner. The dazzling careers of Brooks Robinson and Graig Nettles proved that third basemen aren't all offense.

The same can't be said of most first basemen, who are primarily in the game to hit. And hit. Invariably, sluggers lacking in mobility and flexibility land at first base. That's where fielding throws from the other infielders is their toughest task.

The Yankees' Don Mattingly happens to be equally adept at hitting and fielding, which is saying something considering his consistently terrific batting numbers. Still, some will argue that first basemen aren't really infielders at all, that they are just outfielders who happen to play ninety feet down the right-field line.

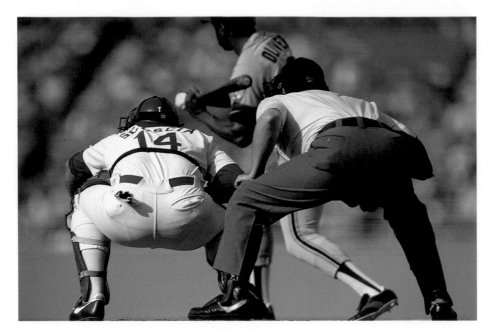

The Catcher

Why, major-league personnel men lament, doesn't anyone want to play this position?

Ted Simmons, who through 1987 had played in 1,762 games behind the plate (sixth on the all-time list), offers an answer: "It hurts when the ball hits you. Who wants to get hurt? It seems like the catcher, more often than not, is the kid who can't do many things real well. But he's willing to pay the price. He's saying, 'Hey, I don't want to sit on the bench. I want to play.' Catcher is the one place you can slide in because nobody else wants to do it."

This is undeniably true, as Ozzie Virgil, most recently of the Atlanta Braves, sees it. His father, Ozzie Sr., played five different positions, including catcher, for nine years in the majors before going into coaching. "My dad watched me as a Little Leaguer," Virgil says. "I was big, had a good arm, and could hit with power, but I couldn't run that fast and I didn't have super good hands. He said, 'We'll put you behind the plate because it's the

fastest way to the majors.' For me, it was probably the only way."

It's a dirty job, but . . . Catchers generally nurse two or three ailments simultaneously, the inevitable result of all those foul tips. They are protected by shin guards, a plastic cup, a chest pad, a mask, and an ability to block out pain entirely. Yet sometimes that defense mechanism doesn't work. How many times have you winced when the catcher grabs one in a delicate region? For many athletes, all the money in the world isn't worth that kind of suffering. And the pain endures: A handshake is an ordeal for many catchers, thanks to disfiguring caused by the steady pounding of a baseball.

The catcher is the most important player on the field day in and day out. He not only touches the ball on every play, but monitors the pitcher's often fragile state of mind, too. One of today's best is Ted Simmons. The powerful switch-hitter was voted to the All-Star Game eight times, based partly on his seven seasons at .300 or better. Yet

CATCHING, AS THE LOS
Angeles Dodgers' Mike Scioscia
(left) will tell you, is grunt work.
Try squatting in your living room
every other half-inning when
watching a game.

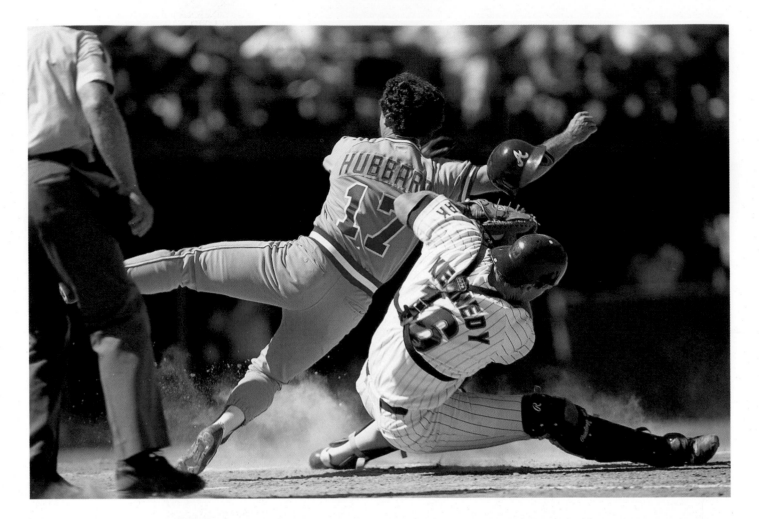

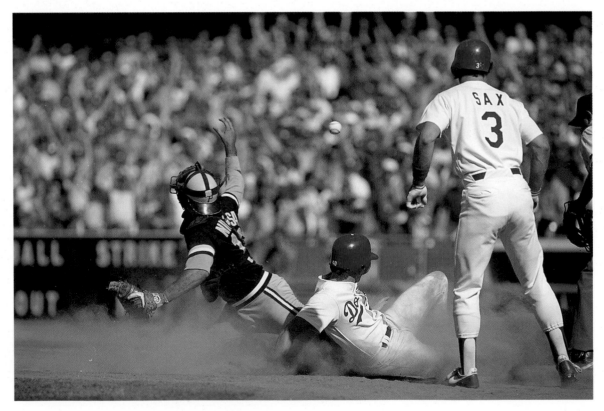

there is no statistic for the rare understanding that Simmons and the game's best catchers bring to each game. Like Simmons, the best catchers are students of humanity who can, on occasion, turn conversation into a metaphysical experience. And they say catchers don the tools of ignorance.

"In a lot of ways, what I do is like an air-traffic controller's job," Simmons says. "It's a lot of responsibility, because you're always making judgments about a pitcher's ability, about his capacity to get the job done in each situation. Objectivity is the prerequisite. You are the manager's alter ego out there. Sure, you're on the pitcher's side, but you are in danger-ous territory when you find yourself hoping and rooting for a guy. They don't always like what I have to tell the manager; like, 'He's not getting it done anymore.' It may be the pitcher's ball, but it's our game to win."

On top of all that, the catcher is the cop of the basepaths, and acts as a deterrent for would-be base stealers. Catcher is such a mentally taxing position that the ones who can hit are often moved to first base, third base, or the outfield, later in their careers. Johnny Bench and Carlton Fisk, two of the best, spent their later seasons at first and third base as well as the outfield. After all that abuse, it's the least a team can do.

THE RUNNER BEARS DOWN on the plate, the ball arrives and . . . he's safe. Surely, there are easier ways to make a living!

The Reliever

KENT TEKULVE, THAT WON-drous sidearmer, was a fixture for the Pittsburgh Pirates from the mid-1970s to the mid-1980s. His ERA was rarely over 3.00. Roger McDowell of the Mets (right) is one of today's best finishers.

Back in Cy Young's day, a pitcher usually finished what he started. Over his career, in fact, Young appeared in 906 games and completed 751 of them, a major-league record. Sparky Lyle, who plied his trade from 1967 to 1982, pitched in 899 games, just behind Young on the all-time list. He didn't go the distance in any of them—because he didn't start any.

Baseball, like everything else, has grown more sophisticated over the years. Lyle is an example of the modern-day specialist: the short man.

Inevitably, a pitcher fades as a game progresses. Forty years ago, he was relieved by a teammate at the bottom of the hierarchy. Players who were struggling as starters, in the manager's doghouse for some reason, or returning from an injury were thrown into the fray. Then one day managers started saving a few arms for the end of games that hung in the balance. Hoyt Wilhelm, who pitched for eight different teams in twenty-one years beginning in 1952, was one of the first who came into prominence. Wilhelm appeared in 1,070 games and won 123 in relief, both all-time standards. The Dodgers were among the leaders in this respect. Ron Perranoski appeared in a league-leading 70 games in 1962, and though his record was a middling 6–6, he entered games in late innings and protected leads 20 times for teammates; this accomplishment became formally known as a save in 1973. As the years passed, the relief plot thickened and pitchers who regularly went the distance grew extinct. Interestingly, no modern pitcher appears among the top 35 in career complete games. Today there are long relievers for those starters knocked from the box early, middle men for three- and four-inning stints, setup men for the critical seventh and eighth innings, and, ultimately, the stopper. This hybrid phenomenon has become baseball's most important position.

Rollie Fingers was the first ultra-modern stopper. He saved a major-league record total of 341 games for the Oakland A's, San Diego Padres, and Milwaukee Brewers between 1968 and 1985, but even he couldn't match Bruce Sutter for sheer consistency.

Sutter was credited 23 saves in 1985, marking the ninth straight year he recorded more than twenty saves. For four straight years, Sutter led the National League, averaging an amazing 31 per season.

Since stoppers generally enter close games, and their margin for error is virtually nothing, they tend to be a little on the bizarre side. "Yeah," says Minnesota's Jeff Reardon, one of the game's premiere finishers, "A lot of relievers are a little goofy. I can see why, with all the pressure on them. Don't believe what a lot of guys tell you—you feel it all the time."

Sutter says one of the keys to success as a reliever is to have a selective memory. "You have to be thick-skinned," says Sutter, "because you'll never be in between. You're either the hero or the goat. Every time you're in the game, it's on the line. You try to forget about it."

FOR A FEW, PRECIOUS YEARS, GOOSE Gossage (left) was baseball's most intimidating force. Reds Manager Pete Rose (above) pulls the plug on another starter and calls for his closer.

Roger McDowell of the Mets has his own thoughts on the subject: "It's a different makeup. You have to have a certain callousness. You're not going to succeed every time. I know I'm not going to win 100 percent of the time, but I know I'll succeed the majority of the time."

In this age of specialization, the stopper almost always has one money pitch that works when he needs it most. Generally, there are men on base, so a consistent strike pitch is required. For McDowell and Reardon, the out pitch is a sinker. Even if the hitter gets his bat on it, the ball is likely to be a grounder, which could lead to a double play. Sutter throws a strange creation known as a split-fingered fastball, baseball's trendiest fashion. In 1973, a coach named Fred Martin taught Sutter how to throw it in the minors. By literally splitting the fingers across the ball's seams, you can throw a pitch that approaches the plate just like a fastball, then dips dramatically at the last moment.

Because a top-notch stopper can appear in nearly half his team's games, the fans tend to lose sight of the big picture. "You reel off six or seven good outings in a row," Reardon says, "then [mess] up once and they'll remember that one for a long time. As a reliever, you really can't win."

That's why they call it a save.

The Pinch-Hitter

Now here is a grim scene: The game is tied and there are two men in scoring position with two out in the top of the ninth. The opposition's best reliever is on the mound and there are 40,000 screaming meanies in the stands. You've been languishing on the bench all this time—muscles atrophying with every inning—watching other people play your position, and now the manager wants you to bail them out. Piece of cake, says Manny Mota, history's most successful pinch-hitter.

"First of all, you must be mentally prepared," says Mota, who amassed 150 pinch-hits in twenty seasons, most of them with the Los Angeles Dodgers. "Never let the manager surprise you. Everybody likes to play every day, but there is a point in your career when you may only hit once a week. You have to put everything into it.

"Concentration and positive thinking are the key. You must have knowledge of the strike zone and be patient. You must have luck. I was the luckiest pinch-hitter ever."

Far from it. Luck, as some season-ticket holder once said, is the residue of busting your butt. Pinch-hitting, as Mota describes it, is a full-time job. "Because you don't hit as often, you have to spend more time in the batting cage working on your timing," he says. "You have to keep your head in the

game, even if you are watching only. You see how they're trying to pitch to a line-drive hitter like you. In my mind, I have a book for every pitcher in the National League; that way, I know what to expect. Then you look at where the outfielders are playing, where the infielders are. This is all necessary because you don't have time to feel sorry for yourself."

Most of the good pinch-hitters learn to subjugate themselves to the team at large. Some (like Mota in his last eight seasons) do it because they can no longer contribute defensively. Others, like Ken Griffey, will do anything to reach the plate and get their rips. Griffey could always hit. For fourteen big-league seasons, his batting average has hovered around the .300 mark. In 1987, the left-hander was thrust into an occasional pinch-hitter's role and thrived. Griffey managed eleven hits in eighteen at-bats for a ridiculous .611 average in the pinch. "Over the years, I've learned to be a contact hitter," Griffey says. "You try not to overswing, try to hit the ball up the middle, go to left field. I try to hang back up there, so I see a lot of changeups. You're just trying to get it in play."

Griffey and Mota are examples of pinch-hitters who are asked only to hit a single. Different situations, however, require different approaches. Smoky Burgess, whose 145 career pinch-hits

are second only to Mota, also managed 126 home runs during his career. Gates Brown, the Detroit slugger who played from 1963 to 1975, was always a threat to hit one out under pressure. Of his 107 career pinch-hits, sixteen were homers. In 1968, on August 9 and 11, Brown hit home runs in consecutive pinch-hit appearances.

Mota, a product of the Dominican

Republic, was himself a fine hitter in an everyday role, though home runs weren't his specialty. He finished his career with a .304 batting average. That his 150 pinch-hits in 505 at-bats works out to .297 is a remarkable tribute to his dedication. Mota says there were times when he came to the plate stiff and out of sync. To loosen up, he claims, "I sometimes swung and missed on purpose. I was always a better hitter when I was behind in the count. With two strikes, you really have to bear down. That's why I don't understand pinch-hitters who get called out on strikes. You have one shot, you've got to swing the bat. You've been waiting for days for the chance; the *worst* thing you can do is take a third strike."

PINCH-HITTING, AS MANNY Mota explains, is mostly about mental preparation. "Never," he says, "let the manager surprise you."

The Base Stealer

VINCE COLEMAN AND WILLIE McGee (below and right) are the cornerstone of the St. Louis Cardinals' good-run, no-hit offense. When they are on the basepaths, speed can kill.

In 1974, Oakland A's owner Charlie O. Finley had an idea. The man who came up with night baseball at the World Series and ill-fated orange baseballs decided that he would invent the designated runner. The designated hitter had been introduced the year before; so why not a designated runner? Surely, there was room for Herb Washington, the world-class sprinter, on Oakland's roster.

Since the man could fly, Finley reasoned, what could be so hard about stealing a base? As it turned out, plenty. "Herb Washington could run as fast as anyone, maybe faster," says Tim Raines, the Montreal Expos outfielder. "But he had one problem—he couldn't steal a base." Well, almost. Washington appeared in 104 games in Finley's two-season experiment, never batted once, and stole thirty-one bases. He

was caught seventeen times, for a dismal success rate of 64.6 percent.

Raines knows something about stealing bases. Through 1987, he had appropriated 511 bases in 585 attempts for history's best percentage, 87.4. He led the National League for four consecutive seasons, from 1981 to 1984. In more than seven seasons in the majors, Raines was thrown out only 37 times by catchers, though he

was picked off by pitchers 36 times. Now, Raines is one of baseball's fastest runners, but clearly there is more to base stealing than just speed.

"It's an art," Raines says. "You have to study a pitcher's habits. What kind of move does he have to first base? Was that first throw over his best? When has he committed to the plate? Are they throwing a pitchout? You've got to think before you even run."

As history's most judicious base stealer, Raines likes to pick his spots carefully. Yet he has stolen seventy or more bases seven different times—another major-league mark. That's one ahead of Rickey Henderson, although there is a good chance that the Yankee outfielder will finish his career as the all-time leader in stolen bases, because he runs with more abandon than Raines. Through 1987, Hender-

son had swiped a staggering 701 bases in less than nine seasons. He was caught stealing 174 times, a success rate of 80 percent.

In 1980, Henderson stole an even 100 bases, third on the all-time list behind Lou Brock's 118 in 1974 and Maury Wills' 104 in 1962. Some opponents felt Henderson was inflating his statistics by running when his team had a big lead. Then, in 1982, the Man of Steal swiped an incredible 130 bases. It may never happen again quite like that. To steal a base, you have to get to first, and Henderson's 143 hits and league-leading 116 walks put him in that position frequently. Henderson would go on to record 108 thefts in 1983 and lead the American League for seven consecutive seasons. Luis Aparicio led the league for nine straight years, 1956-64, but his average take over that period was only 41, reflecting a more conservative time.

There is more to stolen bases than sheer numbers; the mental anguish they cause pitchers and catchers is extraordinary. When the man on the mound throws to first base four or five times to keep the runner close, his concentration is fractured. "You corrupt the pitcher, the whole defense," Raines says. "A situation like that can change the game around. While the pitcher is focusing on you, the advantage goes to the hitter. For one thing, the pitcher's probably not going to be as accurate, which means he can get behind in the count. And with a good runner on, they're going to throw fastballs." When a hitter knows he's going to get a fastball down the middle, watch out.

For more than a hundred years, managers have known the stolen base is one of the game's most exciting and valuable weapons. And in another hundred years, when Herb Washington and orange baseballs are forgotten, they'll still be stealing bases.

IN 1982, RICKY HENDERSON (below), swiped 130 bases for the Oakland A's. No one ever did it better, or is likely to again.

The Umpire

"We are," says Steve Palermo of the American League, "in a no-win situation. There can be 50,000 people in the stands, another 120 million people watching the Series on television, and all it takes is one bad call to get them going.

"Baseball is so many games within a game; there's the cat-and-mouse game between the pitcher and the hitter, and I'm the trap between them. The umpire wins by ensuring that both teams have the same advantages, play by the same rules. It's hard work that's rewarded pretty much with self-satisfaction."

That's about it. When was the last time you heard a standing ovation for an umpire? Pride (and maybe a paycheck) is what gets them through the game. Though some think they are arrogant, frustrated athletes with a dubious sense of humor, good umpires are gifted. They are constantly making decisions that can potentially turn a game, which means they must develop a thick skin.

"You cannot let the crowd intimidate you," says Palermo, considered by many to be the best umpire in baseball. "Personally, I know those boos don't affect me at all. You learn how to handle it. I spent five years in the minors, ten, eleven months a year. You're going to make mistakes, and it can bring you down. Eventually, you get control."

Many players feel umpires have recently begun to exercise too much control. This new aggressiveness

WHEN THE GOING GETS tough, the umpire is likely to be in the middle of it. It takes years of sweat to make it to the major leagues—then you get booed for doing your job.

might be traced to the umpires' strike of 1979, when the men in blue missed seven weeks of the regular season. They walked off the job unified and returned the same way. Time was when a manager like Billy Martin or Earl Weaver could kick dirt on an umpire's shoes and he'd stay in the game. No more. They've always had an argumentative tone, but these days they actually push back on occasion.

Steve Garvey, the gentleman first baseman for the Los Angeles Dodgers and San Diego Padres, was a terrific ballplayer. But as great as his accomplishments were in the field and at bat, he was proudest of his perfect record with respect to umpires: He

was never thrown out of a game—until he was ruled out at the plate in a particularly close play. Garvey, who thought he was safe, yelled over his shoulder to the umpire, "Come on, bear down." He got the thumb. No kidding. Ordinarily, it takes a little more abuse. Umpires don't like to hear the magic word—that twelve-letter one that refers to an Oedipus complex—and they don't like their integrity questioned.

"I was known as one of the biggest red-asses in baseball," Palermo says, "but I've calmed down. But there are times when you have to be a miserable SOB." Still, most umpires manage to find humor in this game.

Eric Gregg of the National League, one of the most enormous men in baseball, likes to tell stories about himself. There was the September 29, 1979, game at Philadelphia when Chicago's Keith Moreland hit a line drive down the left-field line. It might have been foul, but Gregg never really knew. "Sometimes when you look up in the lights, you turn away and see nothing," Gregg says. "Well, that's what happened here. The next thing I see is the ball girl, thigh-high, and she's saying 'Home run, home run.' If it was good enough for her, it was good enough for me."

Another Gregg tale: "I hate Larry Bowa, and this one game at Wrigley

ONCE A FATEFUL CALL HAS
been made, the umpire sometimes
endures a bit of abuse. And some-
times, it's just easier to plug your
ears and not listen at all.

Field I'm working first base and he hits a high chopper. The pitcher and the first baseman and I all collided, and I got knocked out. Just as I'm coming to, Bowa screams, 'Am I out or safe?'

"I go, 'Who's yelling?'"

"He says, 'It's Bowa.'"

"I go, 'You're out!'"

Ron Luciano, a former professional football player, umpired in the American League from 1968 to 1979. He was a character, shooting players with his hand when they were out on the bases and screaming "Outoutout!" In his book, *The Umpire Strikes Back,* Luciano describes some of his experiences, including the 1973 spring training game in which he and Cleveland third baseman Buddy Bell traded places. That's right. Bell was having such a bad day that when he made his third error, he flipped his cap and glove to Luciano and took a position behind third base. Luciano played creditably, even throwing a runner out at second. The runner was actually safe, but second-base umpire Joe Brinkman called him out anyway. You've got to take care of your own.

In 1986, football experimented with the instant replay, and it demonstrated that, generally, referees make good calls. Baseball, conservative game that it is, probably will never take the plunge. The sport just wouldn't be the same. "Who would the ballplayers argue with?" Palermo asks, smiling. "A television camera?"

The Designated Hitter

Since the turn of the century, baseball had hummed fairly quietly on its grand axis. Oh, there had been minor modifications in the game—the infield fly rule was altered slightly in 1901, the strike zone has routinely fluctuated, ground-rule doubles appeared in 1926—but in 1973 the American League got radical. Totally. For 97 years, there were nine men to a side and all of them were responsible for playing both ways. And then the American League, in its collective wisdom, took the bat out of the pitcher's hands. This experiment became known as the Designated Hitter Rule. The National League considered it a travesty, a grotesque departure from the game's genteel sensibilities. The National League was right.

Always looking for a new angle, the American League went too far in its search for more offense. In the mis-

taken belief that baseball fans wanted to see more runs scored—is there anything worse than a sloppy 14–10 ballgame?—the mound already had been lowered five inches four years earlier, which removed some of the pitcher's advantage. The next illogical step was to remove the pitcher from the offense entirely. True enough, pitchers are employed to throw the ball first and hit it last, but the game demands that they step to the plate, even if they depart after three weak swings. History is littered with pitchers who were pathetic standing in against their opposite number. In sixteen years, Detroit's Mickey Lolich hit a robust .110. Hoyt Wilhelm, the knuckleballer of the 1950s and '60s, checked in at .088, while the Yankees' Whitey Ford was 4-for-49 (.082) in eleven World Series. Most pitchers, however, are reasonable athletes.

Some of them actually like to hit. Right hander Burleigh Grimes, who played from 1916 to 1934, was a .248 hitter. In 1925, Walter Johnson managed 42 hits in 97 at-bats, good for a .433 average. Steve Carlton hit three home runs in 1977, the same year he won a league-leading 23 games.

Nevertheless, the American League introduced a non-fielding player to hit for the pitcher. The rule read, in part: *A hitter may be designated to bat for the starting pitcher and all subsequent pitchers in any game without otherwise affecting the status of the pitcher(s) in the game. A DH for the pitcher must be selected prior to the game and must be included in the lineup cards presented to the umpire-in-chief.*

Thus, the face of the game was changed forever. The rule, permanently adopted in 1975, was a boon to

WITH AN AVERAGE THAT hovered around .290, Hal McRae (left) was a designated hitter for most of his career. Boston's Jim Rice (below) played left field for fourteen years before his controversial move to designated hitter.

those good-hit, no-field players who had difficulty landing roster spots because of their liability at first base or in the outfield. Most pitchers average around .190 at the plate, and the designated hitters were immediately more potent, as the league had hoped. The mean batting average was only .270, but teams used the DH in the batting order's power slots and enjoyed dramatically improved run production. But is it baseball?

What does a DH do with his glove if he happens to recognize it lying on the bench? While his fellow batters are out in the field playing defense, the DH can usually be found in the clubhouse riding a stationary bicycle to keep his legs from tightening up. It's a different world. "Everybody's got a different routine," explains Mike Easler, one of the best DHs in the business. "You'll do anything to stay loose. I walk all over the place with a bat in my hands, stretch all the time. You don't think about not playing in the field, because it's your job, a role."

The DH will tell you he'd rather play both ways, but don't believe him. Fielding is boring work, and there's nothing like a little extra time to catch up on your reading. Though the DH rule extended the careers of sluggers like Reggie Jackson and Dave Kingman, there are pitchers like Rick Rhoden of the Yankees who would rather hit himself. A .240 career hitter for the Pirates, Rhoden won three Silver Slugger awards as the National League's best-hitting pitcher.

"I hate the DH," Rhoden freely admits. "First, it slows the game down [pitchers are inevitable rally-enders], and, second, it means some pitchers stay in the game too long. Normally, the manager would take them out, but since he doesn't have to worry about a pinch-hitter, he sometimes leaves them in. That can make for a bad-pitched game. I can't think of anything I like about it."

Amen.

The Plays

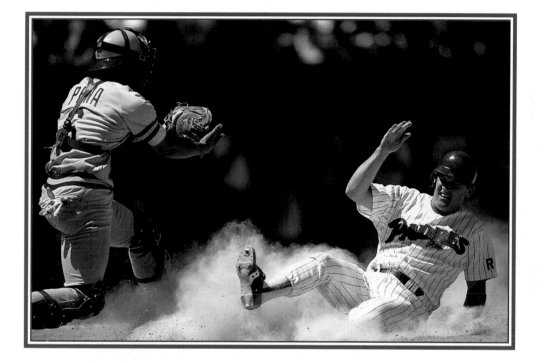

The Home Run

There is something stirring about a home run. Pick a phrase: It is power and glory, good triumphing over evil—unless, of course, your team is in the field. To turn a 90-mile-an-hour fastball back the other way, some 350 feet in the air, is no easy feat. That's why it doesn't happen very often. Even the great Babe Ruth hit only one in every twelve at-bats—and that is baseball's best all-time ratio.

This is why a player drags himself out of bed in the morning, wades through thousands of hours of batting practice in his career, suffers silently in the outfield. "A home run," says slugger Jack Clark, "is an indescribable feeling." No, it doesn't get any

better than this. Unless, of course, you can produce a grand slam. To take the ball out of the park with the bases loaded is a batter's greatest single accomplishment. Lou Gehrig, the old New York Yankee, did it more times (twenty-three) than any other player; Willie McCovey holds on to second place with eighteen. Baltimore's Eddie Murray is the leader among active players, with fourteen through 1987. Though inside-the-park homers may be more exciting to watch, they are often tainted by the artificial turf that makes it possible, or by an outfielder who overruns the ball.

When Hank Aaron closed in on Ruth's all-time mark of 714 home

runs—still the best-known record in all of sport—the attention focused on the Atlanta outfielder in 1974 was unprecedented in baseball. He finished his career with the Milwaukee Brewers, totaling 755 home runs, a number that young fans are already committing to memory. Aaron, like all the great home-run hitters, had terrific timing at the plate and the power to carry fences. Willie Mays (660 homers), Frank Robinson (586), and Harmon Killebrew (573) were the only other players in the ball park.

Naturally, players like to admire their handiwork. Reggie Jackson was noted for his long pauses in the batter's box and the tedious trot that

AFTER HITTING ONE OUT FOR THE DEtroit Tigers, Kirk Gibson (far left) is high on life. Whether they're hit in Boston or Atlanta, home runs are cause for celebration.

inevitably followed. In 1987, Cleveland Indians outfielder Mel Hall hit a tremendous home run, then watched until it cleared the wall at Cleveland Stadium. Teammate Scott Bailes, a pitcher on the bench with nothing better to do, put a stopwatch on Hall and determined that he required 28 seconds to circle the bases, the American League's unofficial season high.

Pitchers, needless to say, aren't in the best frame of mind when they serve up a gopher ball. "It's a bad feeling," says Roger McDowell of the New York Mets. "And when a guy tries to show you up, that just rubs it in. The only thing that feels worse is

walking a guy with the bases loaded with two out in the bottom of the ninth of a tie game—I know, because I did it once in St. Louis." McDowell agrees with most pitchers that the majority of home runs come off bad pitches: fat fastballs out over the plate, hanging curves or sliders. Of course, pitchers will never admit that a hitter sent his best effort into a different zip code.

Home runs come in different sizes and shapes. Jim Rice of the Boston Red Sox, for example, is known for his monstrous line drives. Several minor-league teammates remember a ball he hit 320 feet for a home run that stayed

about five feet off the ground the whole way. This, from a man who has been known to break his bat on checked swings. McDowell's Mets teammate Darryl Strawberry estimates that less than a quarter of his numerous homers are actually well-hit line drives. "Every time you go up, you try to hit a line drive," he says. "But if you just get a hair under it, sometimes it'll go out."

That's right. Many home runs are simply mistakes. "Sometimes, I'd rather hit a line drive than a homer," Jack Clark says, almost convincingly. "Pretty often, a home run is a ball you just missed."

The Triple

This is the purest, most exciting play in baseball. Honest.

Triples are almost always exceedingly well-hit balls in the gaps of the outfield or down the lines. The runner, arms and legs askew, dashes around the bases and crash-lands in a cloud of dust. Triples belong to an older time, before baseball became littered with all those glory-seekers swinging for the fences. Just look at the men who mastered the art.

The first nineteen men on the all-time list played long ago. Stan Musial, at number twenty, is the first modern man on the list—and he campaigned from 1941 to 1963. The greatest triples hitter in history was Samuel Earl Crawford, otherwise known as "Wahoo Sam," owing to his place of birth in Wahoo, Nebraska. Crawford was an even six feet and weighed 190 pounds. He broke into the big leagues in 1899, at the age of nineteen. Cincinnati should have known something was up; in just 31 games, Crawford stroked eight triples. Three years later, the outfielder led the National League for the first time, with 23 three-baggers. In fifteen years with Detroit, Crawford would lead the American League in triples five times. He was a powerful line-drive hitter, who, according to accounts, had pretty fair speed. Crawford retired after the 1917 season with 312 lifetime triples, compared with 97 home runs.

Ty Cobb, the most prolific hitter of all time until Pete Rose, is second on the triples list. He, too, was a line-drive hitter. His 297 career triples dwarfed his home-run production of 118. Third on the list is Honus Wagner, the Pittsburgh shortstop, with 252 triples.

Say what you will about all those old-timers. Believe it or not, each one of the first ten players on the all-time triples list is in the Hall of Fame. A little farther down, you'll find names like (The Immortal) Zack Weat, Elmer Flick, and Shoeless Joe Jackson.

Triples are becoming rarer all the time, for a number of reasons. In the days of Crawford and Cobb, the game wasn't as sophisticated. Smart players could cadge an extra base from unsuspecting outfielders more easily. In 1902, the season that Crawford led the National League with twenty-three triples, the league's eight teams hit a total of 543 triples and only 151 home runs. In 1984, when Ryne Sandberg led the NL with nineteen triples, the twelve-team circuit hit 451 triples—and 1,278 home runs. With more and more hitters swinging with an uppercut in search of home runs, triples hitters have become a vanishing breed.

The National League generally hits more per-capita triples each season. There are two reasons. One, there are more fields covered with artificial turf (six of twelve, in fact). The batted ball actually seems to pick up speed when it bounces off the turf, and that means a lot of hits in the gap dart past outfielders and roll to the wall. Two, National League runners are more often willing to take a chance on the bases, especially when the ball is hit to right-center field.

THE BALL FLIES INTO THE
gap and the batter digs for third.
He's safe in a cloud of dust—one of
the most exciting (and rare) plays
in baseball.

© David Walberg

The Suicide Squeeze

EVEN WHEN A TEAM EX-pects the suicide squeeze, they can still get burned. The Minnesota Twins and St. Louis Cardinals got to the 1987 World Series partially because they understood the subtlety of the squeeze.

Has an ominous tone of finality, doesn't it?

The suicide squeeze is a time-honored, all-or-nothing strategy that merits its own space. Sometimes, in the late innings of a tight game, a manager has no choice but to force the issue. There's a runner on third base, fewer than two outs, and a hitter at the plate who may or may not get that critical base hit. To squeeze or not to squeeze is the silent question the third-base coach asks the manager from along the left-field.

Ozzie Virgil Jr., a National League catcher since 1980, says you can almost smell a suicide squeeze coming. "Suddenly, you notice that something's not right," he says. "If the situation calls for it, you look for the little things. Sometimes you can catch the batter backing off the plate, trying to get the sign from the third-base coach. When he gets it, he's got to acknowledge so the coach can keep the play on and send the runner," Virgil continues. "Then, just as the pitcher's getting ready to release the ball, the hitter will square [to bunt], the runner will take off, and everything starts to happen."

The key is recognition. If the catcher and pitcher can sniff out the squeeze, they can keep the ball away from the hitter, providing the count will allow it. When the suicide squeeze works perfectly, which happens slightly more than half the time, there is nothing a defense can do. If the batter and runner have disguised their intentions sufficiently, the pitcher has already committed himself—he can't appreciably change the direction of the ball. If it's reachable, the hitter must get his bat on the ball and push it back into play somewhere, anywhere. By the time the pitcher, third or first baseman catches up with the ball, the run has scored. Throwing the batter out is little solace. If the hitter misses the ball, the unfortunate

runner will be tagged out easily and a terrific scoring opportunity wasted.

Intuition and good fortune aside, bunting is the skill that makes the suicide squeeze a success. Like breaking up the double play and hitting the cutoff man, bunting is a subtle craft that often goes unnoticed. And unpracticed. Oh, they pay lip service to the bunt in spring training and, yes, the first few pitches in batting practice get nubbed down the first- and third-base lines. Most of today's players, however, don't try to master it.

Phil Rizzuto, the old New York Yankee shortstop, was one of the best. With a lifetime average of .273, he wasn't a real threat with the bat unless he was trying to move someone up on the bases or bunt for an outright hit. Rizzuto would spin to face the pitcher at the last minute, move his hands up the bat head and use his

thumb and index finger to help deaden the ball when it collided with the bat. Touch is everything, and Rizzuto had it. For years, he taught prospective Yankees how to bunt in spring training. Now, when Rizzuto sees a failed bunt from his vantage point in the broadcasting booth, the harangue begins. "These players," he'll moan, "can't bunt today."

Nonetheless, the suicide squeeze remains a part of the game, especially in the National League, where runs are generally harder to come by. The St. Louis Cardinals, with manager Whitey Herzog and his roadrunners, along with the Philadelphia Phillies and Montreal Expos, do it most frequently, perhaps as often as ten times a season. "It isn't a big thing," Virgil says, "but when you execute it right, the other team starts to sag. You've just stolen something that was theirs."

The Brushback Pitch

There was a time when home plate was an equal-opportunity venture: The hitter and pitcher shared it equally. Bob Gibson, the great St. Louis pitcher, liked to say that half of home plate belonged to him—the hitter just had to guess which half. Sal "The Barber" Maglie routinely used to shave the inside edge of the plate. He did it to keep hitters off balance, and keep them honest, too.

It was known as the brushback pitch, the purpose pitch, or chin music. The purpose, apparently, was to scare the living daylights out of potential hitters, making it impossible for them to function successfully at the plate. Remember when a home run meant the next batter would be eating dust? Alas, those days are gone.

"The inside strike has been taken away," says one notable pitcher. "They want to see more runs scored. So hitters are diving inside, throwing themselves into the ball."

Hitters, naturally, suggest this is a cavalier attitude. Certainly, a baseball traveling better than ninety miles an hour can inflict some wicked damage. Yes, careers have been ended. But, as the Yankees' Al Holland points out, pitchers generally aren't trying to hurt anybody. "Why can't we brush them back?" Holland asks. "I'm not talking about hitting them or throwing at their head. But if you can stand up

THE FANGS ARE BARED AND the pitcher lets loose his best weapon—a high, hard one. Batters have no choice but to skip out of the way. Revenge must wait for at least another pitch, unless the hitter wants to charge the mound.

9 0

there and dig in, why can't I knock you on your butt, throw under your chin, and let you know I'm on the mound so that you show me some respect? It ain't about hitting you. It's about getting you off the plate. That's why they're wearing those helmets."

Don Baylor, who has played for five American League teams, has never spent time worrying about pitchers' rights. He has taken more inside pitches on the chin and other exposed areas than any player in baseball history. Baylor is intensely proud of this record—and the fact that, with only one exception, he hasn't allowed opposing pitchers to see him give in to the pain. (A Nolan Ryan fastball is that exception.) "When he gets hit," says former teammate Ken Griffey, "they take the ball out of play." On June 29, 1987—his thirty-eighth birthday—Baylor took a Rick Rhoden fastball on the elbow. He didn't flinch. It was the 244th time Baylor had been hit, one more than Ron Hunt, who had held the record. Baylor feels that by taking the pitcher on, his courage trickles back to the dugout as an example for teammates. And, in his own brave way, Baylor has taken the pitcher's ultimate threat and turned it into an offensive weapon of his own.

The Double Play

There's a runner on first and the number three hitter is at the plate. He rips a shot up the middle just out of the pitcher's reach. With any luck, there will now be runners on first and third with no one out and the cleanup hitter coming up. On the other hand, *sans* luck, if the shortstop can get his glove on the ball, flip it casually to the second baseman, who successfully makes the relay to first base . . . well, it's quite a different story. The cleanup hitter, grumpy because his potential runs-batted-in have been erased, will probably fly to left in frustration. End of inning, courtesy of the dreaded double play. The old two-for-the-price-of-one routine, the twin killing.

How can the unfortunate hitter fall into this trap? Let us count the ways:

"The usual double play is the six-four-three," says shortstop Rafael Santana, the "six" in that familiar score-card combination. "Since most guys are right-handed hitters, they'll pull the ball toward the shortstop. All you've got to do is get the ball cleanly to the second baseman, and then he makes the pivot and the throw. Boom, boom."

Luis Aparicio and Luke Appling, who share several other oddities,

A RUNNER WILL DO ALMOST anything to break up a double-play—legal or not. Here, the Dodgers' Mariano Duncan is able to turn the twin killing (above), even though the runner slides right past the bag in an effort to take him out of the play (right).

helped turn more double plays than any other shortstops. Aparicio, who joined the Chicago White Sox in 1956, was in on 1,553. Appling, who left the White Sox in 1950 and directly follows Aparicio in the *Baseball Encyclopedia,* took part in 1,424 double plays from 1930 to 1950.

Next in popularity is the four-six-three double play, which begins with the second baseman. Over the years, shortstops and second basemen, if they are left together long enough, develop a feeling for where their partner will be on a given play. In some instances, the results can be spectacular. Bill Mazeroski offers a good example of that. Although he was better known for his winning home run in the 1960 World Series, as the Pittsburgh Pirates' second baseman he was involved in a record 1,706 double plays. The majority of double plays are rendered by these middle infielders,

but there are other, less routine ways to double runners up.

Third basemen occasionally start the double play; the Baltimore Orioles' Brooks Robinson—who else?—has the all-time lead with 618. First basemen usually just clean up after the elephants in a double play; Mickey Vernon, who played in the 1940s and '50s, was in on more (2,044) than any man in history. Still, there are times when the first baseman fields a ball off the bag, fires to the shortstop covering second, and accepts the return throw in time to beat the runner. On rare occasions, the catcher will hold onto a third strike, then throw out a runner on the bases, or take a short throw following a bad bunt and relay the ball to first in time to get the runner. Outfielders get into it now and again. Tris Speaker, who played for Boston and Cleveland, threw out 139 runners after recording a putout.

Double plays are usually no accident; they are a calculated risk. The first element is a pitcher, like Tommy John of the New York Yankees, who keeps the ball down or throws a ball that sinks. Infielders love playing behind these pitchers because ground balls are the chief residue. A manager will pull his infielders in toward the plate, along the edge of the grass, in order to increase his chances of turning two. Of course, this gives fielders less time to track a ground ball down. The hitter must oblige with a sharply hit ball; if he doesn't, he's got a chance to beat the play at first base.

Over the years the Boston Red Sox, with all their lead-footed, heavy hitters, traditionally have led the major leagues in hitting into double plays, a dubious honor. With their historical penchant for scraping into position to win it all, then falling tantalizingly short, that is perfectly appropriate.

The Outfield Assist

L en Dykstra, the Mets' fierce center fielder, is getting a little excited here. He's talking about one of his favorite all-time plays. It does not involve a bat. Surprise.

"It's 1986," he says, leaning forward on his clubhouse stool, "and we're out in San Diego. We're in first place, but we need a victory 'cause we're 3,000 miles from home. It's the bottom of the ninth with one out and they've got Garry Templeton on second base. Well, Tim Flannery hits a seed to me in center and it doesn't look too good. Templeton sees it's a hit and heads for home. I let it go and throw him out at the dish. [John] Gibbons is catching—[Gary] Carter is counting his money somewhere—and he goes down when Templeton hits him, but he holds onto the ball. Flannery thinks he's out cold and books for third. Gibbons gets up on his knees and throws him out at third. Double play. Game's over. Weirdest assist I ever had."

Like a lot of outfielders, Dykstra loves to talk about his arm. Perhaps that's because he throws batters out more often than he hits baseballs out of the park. "Sometimes," says New York Mets teammate Darryl Strawberry, noted for prodigious hitting, "a good throw can do as much for you as

a home run. It can really screw up another team's momentum."

In 1883, when runners played fast and loose on the basepaths, a left fielder named Tom Dolan, playing for St. Louis in the American Association, threw out an amazing 62 runners—in 81 games. It stands today as the record, far and away. Still, it was an aberration, because for the remaining four years of his career Dolan was put behind the plate to take better advantage of his arm. Outfielders of that era racked up impressive numbers; Chuck Klein, the Hall of Famer who played from 1928 to 1944, is the only twentieth-century player in the top ten single-season leaders in outfield assists. Tris Speaker (1907–28) is the all-time leader, with 448.

Today's players run with less abandon, affording outfielders fewer opportunities to gun them down. Technically, though, they probably have better arms. Could Dolan possibly have matched the velocity generated by Strawberry or Dave Parker? Not likely. The throwing reputations of these players precede them, leaving them with rare opportunities to show off their arms. Sometimes the best effort of the night is a meaningless throw to second base after a single. In

MANY OF THE BEST OUT-field arms in the major leagues never get tested, because even the speed demons know they'll be gunned down. Here, Jeffrey Leonard makes the throw leading to what is perhaps the play at the plate.

the major leagues, it pays to advertise. Andre Dawson, playing in right field for the Chicago Cubs in 1987, twice threw out pitchers at first base following would-be singles.

For years, Dwight Evans of the Boston Red Sox was one of the game's most highly regarded defensive outfielders. He won eight Gold Glove Awards in right field and had recorded

147 assists through 1987. Through 1987, Dave Winfield of the New York Yankees had produced ten twenty-homer seasons and driven in 100 or more runs six different times, but sometimes he'd rather talk about his seven Gold Gloves. "They say that you're a complete player," Winfield explains. "Every guy likes to think he's well-rounded."

Extra Innings

The Art of Deception

Baseball, by its very nature, is deceitful. They steal bases, don't they? Cheating is not merely tolerated but practiced openly. When there is a runner on second base, the catcher communicates with the pitcher through an elaborate series of signals, lest the hitter be tipped off as to what pitch is coming. Watch a third-base coach during a critical juncture: Facing the batter he touches his letters, his hand goes to his mouth, he tips the bill of his cap, claps, and follows this by a shout of "Come on now, two-eight, let's go to ripping." All of this is necessary to safely convey the manager's orders, through the coach, to the man at the plate. The spies are everywhere. Assistant coaches, whose primary job is hitting fungoes before the game, and utility infielders with nothing better to do in the dugout spend entire games trying to crack the code and turn it to their team's advantage. Remember the old hidden-ball trick? The first baseman fakes a throw back to the pitcher and, if the base runner and first-base coach aren't paying attention, he tags the runner out when he stretches into his lead off first. This is legal—and terribly charming.

Recently, baseball has crossed the line from such roguish behavior to something much more malevolent. Oh, baseball has seen its scandals, large and small. Some of the 1919 Chicago White Sox players threw the World Series against the Cincinnati Reds, and thus were thrown out of baseball for good. In 1970, outfielder Curt Flood, unhappy with a trade from St. Louis to Philadelphia, filed suit against baseball's reserve clause. He ultimately lost when Judge Ben Cooper ruled that federal antitrust laws did not apply to baseball. Two years later, the players struck for the

first time in history, delaying the opening of the season by ten days and causing the cancellation of 86 regular-season games.

Comparatively speaking, the Pine Tar Incident was a breath of fresh air. On July 24, 1983, Kansas City third baseman George Brett, one of the game's great hitters, stroked a home run against Goose Gossage of the New York Yankees. The two-run homer turned a two-out, ninth-inning loss into an apparent 5–4 victory. But the

THESE DAYS, YOU CAN'T trust anybody in baseball. Is there a corked bat among those innocents in the rack? (right) Howard Johnson puts another ball in play with a presumably legal bat.

Yankees, calling on an arcane statute in baseball's rule book that allows no foreign substance more than eighteen inches from the base of the bat, claimed that Brett had too much sticky pine tar on his bat. In fact, the gripping agent was a few inches too high, and though it had no bearing on how far the ball traveled, the Yankees' protest was upheld, Brett's homer was disallowed, and the game was continued a month later. The Royals lost this time. Quite clearly, Brett was not attempting to gain an unfair advantage when he slathered on too much pine tar. The same cannot be said of Billy Hatcher, who was one of the obvious antiheroes when baseball fell from grace in 1987.

Hatcher, an outfielder for the Houston Astros, was suspended after his bat split open and cork was revealed. Partially because home runs were registered at a record pace—there were a staggering 4,458 homers in 1987—many batters were accused of corking their bats. Cork, so the theory goes, lightens the bat head, which allows a hitter to swing it more quickly through the strike zone, which in turn sends the ball farther. Mets infielder Howard Johnson got off to a great start and was dogged by accusations for weeks. There were whispers that other hitters loaded their bats with lead pellets for more hitting punch. Pitchers, too, were the target of accusations.

In the old days, pitchers like Gaylord Perry and Don Sutton were subject to searches on the mound. Perry allegedly liked to slip a little goop on the ball to make it dip like a spitball, while opponents who swung at some of Sutton's stranger offerings and missed claimed he was not above scuffing the ball. Sutton, like Perry, was aware that any small modification of the ball—by addition or subtraction—could drastically affect its flight to the plate. Baseball people suggest that most pitchers cheat at one time or another and that between 20 and 50

percent do so on a regular basis. Although they all staunchly declare their innocence, upon retiring some of the best—like Perry and the Yankees' Whitey Ford—write books and explain in excruciating detail how they cheated. When Sutton was frisked on the mound in 1978, umpires found a note that said, "You're getting warm, but it's still not here!"

The climate in 1987 was anything but laughable. "It's like the witch hunt in Salem," said the Yankees' Tommy John in a typical understatement. "There's a paranoia in the land." Indeed, Kevin Gross, a Phillies pitcher, was suspended when umpires discovered a tack in his glove. The Astros' Mike Scott was the object of several inspections when teams like the New York Mets claimed he was scuffing the ball and offered several oddly defiled balls as evidence. Minnesota Twins knuckleballer Joe Niekro was bitter when umpires searched him during a game against the California Angels. "The first two innings I was struggling my butt off and nobody says anything," Niekro said bitterly. "I finally start getting my knuckleball over and all hell breaks loose." When Niekro emptied his back pockets, an emery board fluttered to the ground. Niekro maintained that he used it to file his nails—essential maintenance for a knuckleballer. But on the mound? The next year, he was handing out emery boards with the legend: "Say it ain't so, Joe—The Niekro File."

As the Yankees' Don Mattingly said at the height of the controversy, "Let the batters load the bats and the pitchers load the ball, and may the best load win."

Baseball management was found guilty of misbehavior as well. Arbitrator Thomas Roberts ruled that major-league owners wrongly acted in concert to shut down the free agent market two years earlier. According to Roberts, the sixty-two players who claimed owners conspired by not offer-

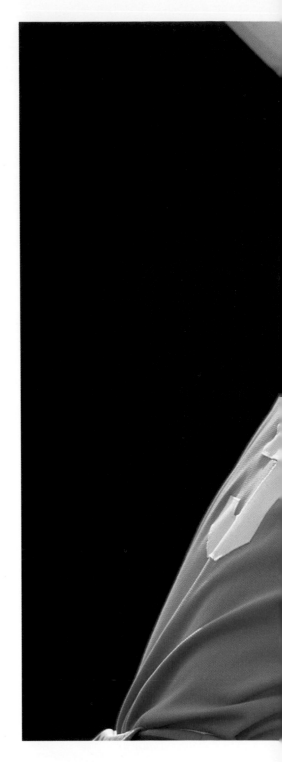

ing free agents lucrative contracts had a valid point; indeed their collective bargaining rights had been violated.

Even the minor leagues weren't immune from the cheating wave. With his Williamsport team twenty-six games out of the pennant race with three to play, catcher Dave Bresnahan made some dubious history. As a Read-

ing base runner moved off third base, Bresnahan pulled a peeled potato from his uniform. He caught the next pitch and intentionally threw the potato over the head of his third baseman. Believing that the ball was flying over his head, the runner lit out for home, only to be tagged by a wickedly grinning Bresnahan, who—wonder of wonders—had the ball in his mitt. No one was amused. The umpire called the runner safe; the Williamsport manager pulled Bresnahan from the game, fined him $50, then sent him walking. The .149 hitter refused to pay the fine, leaving instead fifty potatoes on the manager's desk and a note that read, "This spud's for you."

IT IS LIKELY THAT GEORGE Brett, one of the great hitters of our time, will always be remembered for the Pine Tar Incident.

TWO OF THE BEST MAN-agers in the business: Whitey "The Rat" Herzog of St. Louis and (far right) the Dodgers' Tommy La-sorda. Understanding people is one of the keys to their successes.

The Manager

Through history, some baseball managers have been accorded something approaching cult status: John McGraw, Connie Mack, Casey Stengel, Walter Alston, Earl Weaver, Sparky Anderson, Whitey Herzog. But the nagging question inevitably arises: Do they really make a difference?

Most teams basically play to their ability; that is, the won-lost record reflects the talent level. It is difficult to quantify, but good managers might make a critical difference in ten or so games a year, just as bad managers can have the same impact in a negative way. Invariably, the good ones develop slowly, often beginning as minor-league players who never reach the Big Show. Intelligent players who weren't born with fleet feet or rippling biceps learn how to find that subtle edge. After years of seasoning as a minor-league manager or an assistant coach in the majors, the prospect is ready to run his own shop. And don't think it's all suicide squeezes and hit-and-runs. Managers arc the utility infielders of a team's management; they act as tormentor, psychiatrist, cheerleader, and occasional father figure. Put simply, a manager's job is to intimately understand the peculiar talents of his athletes and put those players in the situations that maximize his team's chance of winning. Piece of cake, right?

Here's Chicago Cubs general manager Dallas Green on his hand-picked choice for manager, Gene Michael: "I think he's done a good job. The key to managing is handling all those 24 people down there, keeping them reasonably happy. I'm not looking for a Little Lord Fauntleroy clubhouse, because controversy in the clubhouse never bothers me. But knowing personalities and personnel to your advantage—that's the key."

As you might imagine, this is vastly easier said than done. High-strung candidates, those A personality types, are going to have problems maintaining an even keel for 162 games a year. Thirty-eight games into the 1987 season, rookie manager Larry Bowa's San Diego Padres were twenty-two games under .500 and fifteen games out of first place in the National League West. "Sleep? You can count the hours I've had on one hand," Bowa said after

the first week. "I've been watching CNN, *Nightline,* X-rated movies. I'm going all night. By the time I finally go to sleep, I wake up and it's 4:30 and I'm trying to make another lineup. These have been the most miserable days of my life." A few weeks later, Bowa was wearing Band-Aids on two of his fingers because he had chewed the nails to the quick. In less than a month, Bowa had alienated most of his young team. Center fielder Stanley Jefferson had to be dragged by five teammates from Bowa's office at Three Rivers Stadium in Pittsburgh. Billy Martin, another volatile sort, set a record in 1988 when he became the New York Yankees' manager for the fifth time. Over the years, he has had

numerous altercations in bars and, on one bizarre occasion, an ugly dispute with a marshmallow salesman.

These days, the best manager in baseball is named Dorrel Norman Elvert Herzog. His friends call him Whitey or the White Rat. In any case, Herzog is the prototypical modern manager. According to a recent poll of major-league general managers, he is the man they would most want guiding their team.

How did Herzog gain this rare insight? By occupying virtually every job baseball has to offer. Herzog was originally signed by the New York Yankees in 1949 out of New Athens (IL) High School. They were under the impression he was an outfielder, so Herzog

kicked around the minors as an outfielder who could hit a little. He eventually matriculated to the Washington Senators, where he hit .232 for two seasons. In all, Herzog was traded three times and sold outright once, to the Kansas City Athletics. He became an assistant coach there and, after tours of duty at Texas and California, returned to manage the Royals in 1975. In four full seasons, Herzog's team finished first three times and second once. It was in Kansas City, where his record was 410–304, that Herzog first began to meld his version of baseball with the environment of artificial turf, which requires speed at almost every position. Herzog took over a Cardinals team that started the

GENE MAUCH, BILLY MARTIN, PETE ROSE
. . . all three played in the Big Leagues (with varying results) and all three made the transition to managing.

1980 season 19–34 under Ken Boyer, and through 1987 his team had been to the World Series three times. When Herzog's team moved into the Mets' former facility in St. Petersburg in 1988, Herzog explained his *modus operandi* in a talk with neighborhood fans: "You don't have to take out insurance, because I don't have too many guys who can reach your houses. But if you steal baseballs, I've got guys who can catch you."

Since Herzog has seen virtually everything, he has a lot of options. He once fielded a lineup that featured six switch-hitters, and said he could have used more. On many occasions, Herzog keeps his pitchers in the game by playing one in the outfield while another comes in to handle a particularly tough hitter. Strategy aside, Herzog listens to his players. When rumors flew during the 1987 off-season that third baseman Terry Pendleton would

be traded to the Montreal Expos, Herzog met with Pendleton and told him he'd be with the Cardinals at least through the next season, though he couldn't guarantee anything beyond that. Pendleton, relieved and appreciative of Herzog's candor, had the best year of his career.

The 1986 World Series between the Red Sox and Mets offered an interesting contrast with respect to managers. Red Sox pilot John McNamara played catcher for fourteen seasons in the minor leagues and hit a resounding .239. Still, he maneuvered Boston and its spotty pitching rotation into the Fall Classic. Mets manager Davey Johnson was a gifted major-league player. He appeared in three All-Star games with the Orioles and, in 1973, hit forty-three home runs for Atlanta, breaking Rogers Hornsby's record for second basemen. Yet Johnson was not too big to miss the game's nuances. His successful platooning of players was one of the chief reasons the Mets overcame the Red Sox in seven games after trailing 5–3 in the sixth contest with two outs and two strikes on third baseman Ray Knight. When Johnson was playing for Weaver in Baltimore he had, in fact, first begun to use a computer to chart tendencies.

Who was the best in history? Connie Mack, who managed for an amazing fifty-three years, has the most games (7,878), wins (3,776) and loses (4,025), despite the fact that Philadelphia teams weren't particularly gifted. Joe McCarthy, the Yankees' skipper from 1931 to 1946, won 2,126 of 3,489 games, a winning percentage of .614, the all-time best. McCarthy was also 30–13 (.698) in nine World Series, another record. But, of course, he had players like Babe Ruth and Lou Gehrig in the lineup. Outfielder Claudell Washington, who played for a few managers in his day, says: "A guy's only as good as the players he has. The real good ones can make you think you're better than you are, or worse. That's what managers really do."

The Strategy

Baseball is a game of choices, with plenty of time built in to exercise those options. *Strategy* is the so-called logic behind those choices. Consider the Milwaukee Brewers' unique defense, unveiled on June 29, 1987:

Detroit Tigers catcher Matt Nokes came to the plate in the fifth inning, with the Brewers trailing 5–0 and runners on second and third. Milwaukee manager Tom Trebelhorn summoned Robin Yount from center field and positioned him in the middle of the infield, leaving the Brewers with two outfielders. Nokes bounced back to pitcher John Henry Johnson and the runners failed to advance. Presumably flushed with success, Trebelhorn waved in right fielder Rob Deer to play alongside Yount as Pat Sheridan stepped to the plate. That meant the Brewers were playing six infielders—something veteran observers could not remember happening before—and Mike Felder was the lone outfielder. "I

thought I was back on a football kickoff return team," Felder said later. "As I looked in, I saw a wedge setting up for me. I was looking for a few blocks." Sheridan ruined the strategy by hitting a single to right-center that skipped just in front of Felder and drove in the game's sixth run. Later, Trebelhorn explained that the scouts had noticed Sheridan's propensity for taking left-handed pitchers up the middle along the ground. Oh. The Brewers eventually lost the game, 11–0.

Most strategy is more conventional. The cardinal rule is that managers would prefer to have left-handed pitchers throwing to left-handed batters, and righties facing right-handed hitters. This is because then the pitcher's throwing arm and the hitter's body are on the same side of home plate. The curveball, for instance, starts in the batter's face and veers away over the plate—if it breaks at all. Many hitters aren't willing to

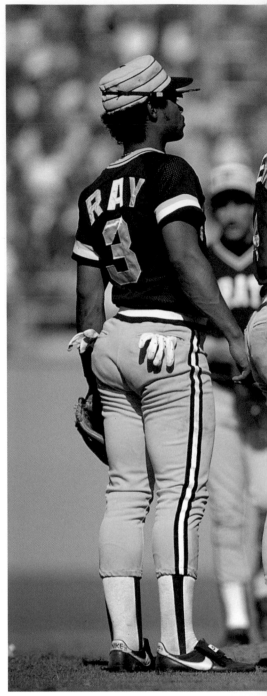

RUSTY STAUB MAKES A point (left), while Chuck Tanner presides over a summit meeting in Pittsburgh. Is Tanner asking about the party after the game?

take that on faith. Years ago, managers discovered that by starting a runner off first base, a hole opened up when the shortstop or second baseman ran to cover second. It's called the hit-and-run, and infielders take great pains to disguise who will cover the bag, forcing the hitter to guess which side will be vacated.

Strategy is, in large part, based on history, on tendencies. Does this right-handed hitter look for breaking stuff when he's ahead in the count? Is this base runner more of a threat to run when the count is two-and-one or one-and-two? Will a pitchout change his mind? Hitter A hits the daylights out of Pitcher B, so how to arrange a confrontation? Managers, in fact, spend a great deal of time maneuvering to get the individual matchups they want.

Often, strategy is an extention of a manager's particular style. The Cardinals' Whitey Herzog loves to manufacture runs with the hit-and-run and stolen bases. He occasionally hides his pitchers in the outfield between stints on the mound. Earl Weaver of the Baltimore Orioles used the Big Bang Theory: He wanted his slugger at the plate with men on base. Sometimes strategy is merely instinct. The facts at hand may not support the decision, but a manager learns to trust these twinges of intuition. Quite often these hunches work. Sometimes they do not. In 1980, the Los Angeles Dodgers and Houston Astros met in a one-game playoff for the National League West title. Dodger manager Tommy Lasorda had to make a choice between nine-year veteran Dave Goltz, a 7–10 right-hander who had led the league in hits allowed two of the previous three years, and a 2–0 rookie named Fernando Valenzuela, who hadn't allowed an earned run in ten appearances. Unfortunately for Lasorda, he went with Goltz and the Dodgers lost in convincing fashion.

Win some, lose some.

The Fan

BEING THERE IS THE WHOLE idea in baseball. Fans flocked to the stadiums in 1987—more than ever before—to be part of the action.

In 1987, more than 52 million fans attended major-league baseball games; millions more watch regularly on television. What is it that makes baseball the popular sport it is, the undeniable national pastime?

"Baseball has been around for a hundred years," says Rod Heffern, general manager of the Baseball Card Store in Plantation, Florida. "It has a sense of history. I mean, they were rooting for professional clubs in places like Toledo, Ohio, back in the late 1800s. This is the last vestige of true heroes. A guy steps up to the plate, and if he can dig down in his soul, no matter what the odds are, he can hit it over the fence. People can identify with that."

They stream into Heffern's store all year long: The snowbirds from New York during spring training (the Yankees work about ten miles away in Fort Lauderdale), the kids on spring break, the collectors during the long, hot summer. Most of them are fans, Heffern says: "Some of them just like to shoot the breeze. Time goes by fast when you're talking baseball." Most of these followers have no idea how valuable some of these cards are, like the Honus Wagner T-206. In the early 1900s, Piedmont cigarettes printed cards bearing pictures of baseball players on the back of their packs. Wagner, who didn't condone smoking, asked that his cards be destroyed. Only thirty exist today, and they're worth

$100,000 each. Real fans don't hunger for Mickey Mantle's rookie card of 1952, worth $6,000 in some circles, or those precious cards of Ruth and Gehrig. It's the Diego Seguis and the Jerry Hairstons of the world that they truly cherish.

Baseball thrives, in part, because it is an individual sport. A pitcher has eight defenders with him out on the field, but sometimes the mound can be a lonely place. There's no place to hide when the hitter wins this battle and that home run clears the left-field fence. No other team sport consistently offers as many dramatic one-on-one confrontations. It is a game equally appealing to the masses and the literati. Hemingway loved the game, and there have been numerous novels about the baseball experience. Roger Angell, of *The New Yorker,* is baseball's most eloquent observer today. A. Bartlett Giamatti, a scholar in the field of Renaissance literature, retired as president of Yale University in 1986 to become president of the National League. His treatises over the years have carried titles like "The Green Fields of the Mind" and "Baseball and the American Character."

Fans are everywhere. Richard Nixon was fascinated by the game. Most

In many families, baseball is handed down from generation to generation. It starts with a child's first major-league baseball game, an extraordinarily important event for the father. He or she learns the players' names and the intricacies of the scorecard, which leaves a wide margin for individualism—ask three people how they score a bunt single and you may get three different answers. It's a highly personal matter. These F-7s and 4-3s will rest in storage, suspended in limbo, until they are recalled at a later day. There are autographs and photographs, caps and pennants. Is there any treasure greater than an autographed baseball? Then, when the wheel turns completely, another generation is indoctrinated.

A TRUE FAN WILL GO TO ANY LENGTH TO GET A SOUVENIR.
Others prefer to just root for their team and enjoy America's pastime.

sportswriters who cover baseball are passionate fans, though they will deny it. Then there is Joseph Reichler, whose *Baseball Encyclopedia* is a dog-eared staple for many fans. His labor is clearly one of love. The same goes for the statistical maniacs at the Elias Sports Bureau in New York City. They don't just provide numbers for the media, they offer unsolicited opinions on the figures' deeper meanings.

The Wildlife

Baseball supports a number of minor characters, who step in on those occasions when the game lags.

The organists keep the crowd involved with background music, often with appropriate titles for the particular moment—although "Raindrops Keep Falling on My Head" gets a little old during rain delays. These keyboardists are sometimes the most important element in a rally, inducing fans to clap rhythmically or favor their heroes with a "Charge!" There are colorful public address men like John Miller in Baltimore, who can mimic any famous announcer. Those ball girls who sit on stools down the right- and left-field lines don't serve any functional purpose, but they do improve the scenery, which is the point. Even baseball's button-down purists concede that ball girls are an innovation they can live with—yet mention some of the mascots around the major leagues, and they cringe.

Admittedly, some mascots are better than others. The Montreal Expos have a huge orange creature named Youppi, who vaguely resembles a bear. People in the Expos' front office aren't quite sure what it is.

Q: "What, exactly, is he?"

A: "First of all, I'm not sure it's a he; secondly, I have no idea."

Youppi seems to have that effect on people. The Phillie Phanatic, another strange, fuzzy animal, has quite a few good moves. Inside, David Raymond, the son of Delaware football coach Tubby Raymond, sweats like a madman while he entertains the crowd with a well-rounded act. The Pittsburgh Pirates have a likable parrot, but the best bird or beast in the game is The Famous Chicken, who is based in San Diego.

Most mascots in the sporting world have borrowed part of their act from

TONY GWYNN AND TIM FLANnery (far left) consistently reel them in around San Diego; while Dan Driessen (above) fields a high hopper and Terry Kennedy (left) shows what is on his mind.

The Chicken. "I don't have a lot of respect for a lot of those other creatures," concedes Ted Giannoulas, The Chicken's alter ego. "There are a lot of rip-off artists out there."

Giannoulas was minding his own business in 1974, studying journalism at San Diego State, when a representative of radio station KGB entered the campus radio station looking for a volunteer. KGB had a deal: In exchange for wearing a chicken suit and handing out Easter eggs at the San Diego Zoo, they were offering $2 an hour. Unaware that California's minimum wage was $2.25 at the time, the five-foot-four Giannoulas was the instant choice. He handled the job for a week, then talked the station and the Padres into letting him attend games at Jack Murphy Stadium. The Chicken was a hit. He had a sense of humor. Even Pete Rose had to laugh when Giannoulas ran to first base after a walk, tore around the bases, flew into third base with Rose's trademark

head-first slide, then did a sort of slow-motion, Sam Peckinpah version of Rose's All-Star Game collision with Ray Fosse. The Chicken would dress up as a doctor and offer umpires a physical examination. At coach Roger Craig's suggestion, Giannoulas produced an eye chart as the classic gag's punch line. The Chicken's reputation grew and, after surviving a messy $250,000 lawsuit with the radio station because, says Giannoulas, "My career ambitions conflicted with their policies," he became a freelancer.

The Chicken works some 250 dates a year, more than half of them baseball games. He's been all over the country, as well as Mexico, Japan, and Australia. Giannoulas says he has about a hundred routines, though not everyone laughs along with him. One journeyman pitcher hit a home run in an old-timer's game and, when The Chicken attempted to halt his progress around third base, went into a fullback stance and knocked him out of the way. In the

WHEN THE CHICKEN IS ON hand, a baseball game becomes one big party.

process, the pitcher dislocated his non-pitching shoulder and landed on the disabled list for two weeks. Giannoulas lost his lawsuit, too.

Giannoulas says he is quite aware of where The Chicken's personality ends and his begins. "They're really quite distinct, there's no blur," he says. "I'm mild-mannered, but when I put on that second skin, it's a Jekyll-and-Hyde thing. The laughter of the fans is

a great aphrodisiac." And the pay is better than $2 an hour.

Morgana, the kissing bandit, works baseball games for free. In real life, she's a stripper with enormous, uh, tassels. Her shtick is to enter the ball park incognito, then burst onto the field and hug her victim. Then there is Wild Bill Hagy, who rose to prominence in 1983, when the Orioles won the World Series. Hagy used his entire

body to spell O-R-I-O-L-E-S, and soon it caught on with the fans. In one tender tribute, the entire Baltimore team took the field and spelled right along with him. And then there is the peanut vendor in Los Angeles who rivals Ozzie Smith with some of his creative throws, or the resident sign-makers in many parks. They're all part of baseball's colorful landscape, wildlife at the fringes of the game.

The Classics

The World Series

Based on the regular-season results of 1987, the Minnesota Twins did not exactly belong in the American League Championship Series. So what were they doing in the World Series?

The Twinkies were 85–77, winning the West Division by a scant two games over Kansas City. That .525 winning percentage—the worst ever by an eventual World Series winner— would have netted them fifth place in

the East Division, some thirteen-and-a-half games behind the Detroit Tigers. Minnesota was ranked tenth among the fourteen American League teams in both batting and pitching. Naturally, the Twins blasted the Tigers four games to one in the playoffs and prepared to host the St. Louis Cardinals in the 85th summit conference between the American and National League champions. And that was the

whole trick. During the regular season, the Twins lost 52 of 81 games on the road, a staggering number. Conversely, Minnesota was 56-25 at home in the Hubert H. Humphrey Metrodome. For some reason, the Twins could play in this eerily lit, surreal structure supported by hot air. More importantly, visiting teams could not.

"Something about it," says Twins outfielder Tom Brunansky. "I think

TERRY PENDLETON WAS
thrilled when the St. Louis Cardi-
nals advanced to the 1987 World
Series, despite what some San
Francisco Giants fans thought.

the building intimidates some teams. They come in saying, 'We're not going to play well here.' And then that's just what happens."

And so the World Series moved inside for the first time in history. It was different, that's for sure. The Metrodome's fences look like plastic garbage bags and, though they're positioned a creditable distance from the plate, baseballs fly over them with appalling ease. The Cardinals were a team built for this bouncy, artificial turf, but they had never seen 55,000 loonies waving Homer Hankies—and they had never heard the kind of enclosed roar that eventually knocked out ABC Television's decibel meter. Not before, we should point out, the roar had surpassed the sound of a jet airplane. The Cards, without their disabled slugger Jack Clark, never had a chance.

One reason teams reach the World Series is their comfort level at home; in 1987 the Twins and Cardinals proved emphatically to be products of their environment. Neither team won a game in the other's park. "That's the trouble with molding a team to its park," says Yankee second baseman Willie Randolph, who played in three

World Series between 1976 and 1981. "You can get lost on the road."

Minnesota bombed St. Louis 10-1 in the opener and 8-4 before heading to Busch Stadium. The Cardinals, relying on pitching and wily manager Whitey Herzog, came back and dusted the Twins in three straight at home. The running of Vince Coleman and the defensive wizardry of shortstop Ozzie Smith compensated for no visible means of hitting. Outscored 14–5 in St. Louis, Minnesota won game six 11–

5 in part due to Kent Hrbek's 439 foot grand slam. The seventh game was predictably devoid of drama. The Twins won going away, 4–2, and were annointed champions of the world.

Four months later, toiling at spring training in Orlando, Florida, the players said it was like it never happened. "Unreal," reliever Jeff Reardon said, stretching the arm he used to mesmerize the Cardinals. "You're there, but you're not really sure you have control of what's going on."

Even more than a year after the New York Mets' 1986 World Series win, Roger McDowell, Reardon's successful counterpart that year, had difficulty describing the experience. "You know you're one of the best two teams in baseball," he said, "but it wasn't an enjoyable time, really. There's so much pressure. All these people you know want to come see it, so you've got to get them tickets and you have to worry about getting them to the ballpark, figuring out where they're

KIRBY PUCKETT, KENT Hrbek, and Frank Viola (left to right) helped the Minnesota Twins prevail over the St. Louis Cardinals in a loud, loud series.

going to stay. And then you get to the stadium and there's this intensity in every game, every inning, every pitch. It's hard to absorb. After we beat the Red Sox, I got a videotape of the year in review. I played it just the other day. Smokey Robinson sang the National Anthem and kind of blended it with 'America the Beautiful.' It was like, man, did that really happen?"

The Cardinals were asking the same question after the Twins beat them a year later. Since it takes four games to win, the World Series doesn't suffer from one-game, one-sided disasters like so many recent Super Bowls. You get to come back. That's one reason World Series are a lot like television's mini-series: Quite often there are some strange turns of plot.

Some of the highlights over the years have included the following:

• The New York Giants may have swept their 1954 Series with the Cleveland Indians in four games, but who remembers that? This was the year Willie Mays made not one but two spectacular catches on Vic Wertz in the first game. Many feel the first grab, a full-speed, over-the-shoulder basket catch of a 460-foot blow to deepest center field at the Polo Grounds, was baseball's greatest catch ever, under the circumstances. Although Mays saved two runs and preserved an eighth-inning tie, he always maintained his toughest chance of the Series came in the tenth inning of the same game when he made a back-handed stab of Wertz' line drive to left-center field. Wertz was left on second and, in the bottom of the frame, Mays scored the winning run on Dusty Rhodes' three-run home run.

• Two seasons earlier, the New York Yankees' pedestrian right-handed pitcher had led the American League with twenty-one losses, but in 1956 Don Larsen outshone stars like Whitey Ford, Mickey Mantle, Yogi Berra, Roy Campanella, Jackie Robinson, and Gil Hodges. With the Series tied at two games apiece, Larsen threw an utterly perfect game at the Los Angeles Dodgers. He needed ninety-seven pitches to record the only no-hit, no-walk, no-run game in World Series history. The Yankees won in seven games; in ten subsequent seasons, Larsen would be an even .500 pitcher.

• It was the seventh game of the 1960 World Series, and Yankee right-hander Ralph Terry was trying to force the Pittsburgh Pirates into extra innings in this ultimate contest. Bill Mazeroski's specialty was fastballs and, oddly enough, one came toward the plate as he led off the ninth. The second baseman made a mental note and watched it go by. The second pitch was in the same spot, only slightly lower. Mazeroski hit it over the fence in left-center at Forbes Field. The Pirates won, 10-9, and Mazeroski was a hero for the ages.

© David Walberg

• Though they had finished ninth, at 73–89, the year before, the 1969 New York Mets had tenacity. They trailed the Chicago Cubs by nine-and-a-half games on Aug. 13, but won 38 of their final 49 games to win the National League East Division by eight games. The 109–53 Baltimore Orioles, champions of the American League, hardly gave them a second thought. Amazingly enough, the Mets won in four straight games, recording one of the greatest upsets in history.

• Even the old-timers who vaguely remembered Boston's victory over Pittsburgh in the inaugural 1903 World Series had to admit that the 1975 version was something special. The sixth game was the most memorable, because the Red Sox evened the Series with Cincinnati at three-all with some ferocious shots in the dark. First, Bernie Carbo hit a pinch-hit, three-run homer to tie the game at 6–6 in the eighth inning. Then came Carlton Fisk's frozen-in-memory home run off the foul pole in left field, which ended the game in twelve innings. The Reds' Joe Morgan singled with two out in the ninth one night later to carry Cincinnati to a 4–3 victory in anticlimactic fashion, for game six was a tough act to follow. Perhaps the toughest.

THE CARDINALS, INCLUDING Willie McGee (far left), could never quite catch the Twins, and when it was all over Kirby Puckett (above) was one happy guy.

123

The All-Star Game

It is a midsummer night's dream, a gathering of—with a few annual exceptions—baseball's finest talent. The All-Star Game sprung from the fertile mind of Chicago Tribune sports editor Arch Ward, who also conceived the College All-Star Football Game and the Golden Gloves boxing tournament. Baseball, like the rest of the nation, was going through a depressing economic period in the 1930s. This "Game of the Century" between the National and American Leagues was Ward's idea to raise money for former ballplayers who needed assistance. Initially, the All-Star Game was merely a warmup act for the 1933 Century of Progress Exposition in Chi-

cago. More than fifty years later, tens of millions of television viewers tune in to the spectacle—perhaps because they have a personal investment.

Although Ward chose the managers for the inaugural game—Connie Mack and John McGraw, who had met previously in some memorable World Series—the fans were permitted to select the players. Well, in a way. The Tribune printed eighteen-player ballots in some of the country's great newspapers, but most returns came from the Chicago area. The managers, armed with these results, actually had the power to chose anyone they wanted. After two years of this system, the eight managers from each

league were awarded the task of choosing sides. And though managers are more in touch with who is having a good season and who isn't, the vote was returned to the fans in 1947, after twelve seasons. Baseball's brain trust understood quite well on which side its bread was buttered. Unfortunately, the fans in Cincinnati got a little overzealous in 1957. Just a tad. More than a half-million late votes from the Redlegs' fans ensured that the entire Cincinnati starting lineup, with the exception of first baseman George Crowe, would be on the field at Busch Stadium in St. Louis. Baseball Commissioner Ford Frick was not amused; he took the vote away from the fans,

who clearly could not handle the awesome responsibility. In 1970, Commissioner Bowie Kuhn, in a public relations coup, gave the fans their votes back and, for the most part, they have behaved themselves ever since. Recently, All-Star voting has grown into the nation's largest nonpolitical election. The top players consistently draw more than three million votes, more than some celebrated independents in Presidential elections. You could look it up.

Not that there aren't a few problems with this multicolored, multilayered classic. One built-in drawback to the balloting system is the treatment of rookies. How can baseball predict how a first-year player's season will go? Nevertheless, names like Kelly Gruber, Edgar Diaz, and Robby Nelson appear alongside those of Winfield, Schmidt,

THE ALL-STAR GAME IS about stars. For several years, St. Louis shortstop Ozzie Smith (left) has been the fans' biggest vote-getter. Oakland's Jose Canseco (above) is a new star, while Boston's Wade Boggs (right) is a perennial bat in the American League lineup.

and Hernandez. When someone like Oakland A's first baseman Mark McGuire opens the season with a blinding stretch of hitting, he must make the team as a write-in candidate. And then there are those players who remain unmoved by the pomp and circumstance: They would rather skip the three-day affair and go fishing. Every year, one or two players beg off with some nagging injury, or a 14–2 hurler declines his invitation because the pitching rotation won't permit him to throw twice in three days. Pity.

Fortunately, most players understand that their All-Star selection is an honor—and they also understand that the fans tend to be a little sentimental in their voting. Yet more often than not, the players play with inspiration:

• Babe Ruth, clearly past his prime at the age of thirty-eight, was the leading vote-getter in the first All-Star Game in 1933, garnering some 10,000 ballots. Before a crowd of 47,000 at Chicago's Comiskey Park, Ruth led the American League to victory with a resounding two-run homer and made a great catch on Chick Hafey's long drive to the fence in right field. Ruth's epic performance was one reason the All-Star Game has become the leading such gathering in all of sports.

• At least early on, the National League suffered at the hands of its American League brethren. The AL had won four times, to the NL's one, when Leo "The Lip" Durocher turned a 30-foot bunt into a four-base circus at Crosley Field in Cincinnati in 1938. With the Nationals leading by a tenuous 2–0 score, Frank McCormick led off the seventh with a single off Lefty Grove. Durocher was instructed to bunt by manager Bill Terry. This he did, pushing a little squibber down the third-base line. Jimmie Foxx made a clean play and threw to first, but Charlie Gehringer wasn't covering and the ball wound up in right field. McCormick headed for the plate, and Joe DiMaggio's throw flew over the head

of catcher Bill Dickey and into the opposing dugout. Durocher scored, and the Nationals went on to score a psyche-lifting 4–1 victory.

• Ted Williams' 1941 season was memorable for several reasons, not the least of which was his .406 batting average, the last .400 season the majors ever saw. In the All-Star Game at Detroit's Briggs Stadium, Williams

won the game in dramatic fashion. With the American league trailing 5–4 with two outs in the ninth, Williams hit Claude Passeau's two-and-one offering some 450 feet for a home run—it would have traveled more than 500 feet if the facade of the third tier hadn't interfered.

• The All-Star Game is an exhibition of sorts, but Pete Rose never felt

THE YANKEES' DON MAT-
tingly (left) and Darryl Strawberry
(right) of the Mets are two of the
most popular players in New York
and are annual entries in the All-
Star Game. This may continue in-
definitely.

that way. On display before the home crowd in brand-new Riverfront Stadium in Cincinnati, Rose won the 1970 game in the twelfth inning with the kind of effort that inspired the nickname "Charlie Hustle." The game was tied at four-all when Rose singled to center with two out and Billy Grabarkewitz followed suit. Jim Hickman singled to center, and Rose never slowed down rounding third base. He met catcher Ray Fosse, a good friend of his off the field, a few feet from the plate in a sickening collision. Rose arrived just ahead of the ball, which Fosse never handled. The Nationals won, 5-4.

There were other great moments in All-Star history—Carl Hubbell's five consecutive strikeouts of Babe Ruth, Lou Gehrig, Jimmie Foxx, Al Simmons, and Joe Cronin in 1934; Johnny

Callison's game-saving homer for the Nationals with two outs and two strikes in 1964; Reggie Jackson's monstrous 520-foot shot in 1971 that hit a light tower in deep right field at Tiger Stadium—but recently a nagging question has surfaced. Why can't the American Leaguers beat the Nationals anymore? Since evening the series at seventeen-all in 1964, the National League has won 20 of 23 contests through 1987, including a startling string of eleven straight from 1972–82.

The American League uses words like "fluke" and "coincidence," but clearly something is happening here. There are several theories. Through the '70s, the National League had a good-sized core of repeat players who seemed to mesh well together. Another factor is the National League's tighter, more efficient style of play, which features aggressive baserunning and tends to succeed in one-game meetings. Perhaps, at bottom, the National League takes the game more seriously. League president Warren Giles was above motivational speeches, which might partially explain the one-sided results of late. Outfielder Dave Winfield, who has played both sides of the fence, for the San Diego Padres and the New York Yankees, says he noticed a difference when he moved to the American

League. "Before the game, the National League players would meet and talk about strategy," Winfield says. "The American League players just show up and go out to play. It meant more to us in the National League." The American League players get defensive and claim the All-Star Game is only an exhibition. They point to five consecutive victories in the World Series. In this midsummer classic, at least, the American stars don't come out often enough.

MORE COMMONLY A THIRD baseman, the Brewers' Paul Molitor played at second base for the American League in the 1988 All-Star game. It is not uncommon for several players—usually outfielders —to play out of position in the All-Star game because of the fans' tendency to vote for their favorites, regardless of position.